CHOOSING LIFE

CHOOSING LIFE

by

John English, S.J.

PAULIST PRESS
New York/Ramsey/Toronto

ACKNOWLEDGEMENTS

All scriptural quotations, unless otherwise indicated, are from *The Jerusalem Bible*, Doubleday & Co., Inc., Garden City, N.Y. 1966.

All quotations from The *Spiritual Exercise of St. Ignatius* are from the edition of Newman Press, Westminster, 1951, translated by Louis Puhl, S.J. These quotations are always marked off with square brackets.

Quotations from the decrees of Vatican Council II are from *The Documents of Vatican II*, America Press, New York, 1966.

CENSORS LIBRORUM

Rev. Thomas F. Walsh, S.J.
Rector, St. Ignatius Loyola Parish, New York

Rev. M.J. Belair, S.J.
Rector, Loyola Jesuit Community, Montreal

IMPRIMI POTEST
Rev. Terence G. Walsh, S.J.
Provincial, Toronto

March 15, 1978

Library of Congress
Catalog Card Number: 78-58315

ISBN: 0-8091-2113-1

Published by Paulist Press
Editorial Office: 1865 Broadway, New York, N.Y. 10023
Business Office: 545 Island Road, Ramsey, N.J. 07446

Printed and bound in the
United States of America

CONTENTS

To
Len, Dessa, Mary,
Alex, Diane, George
and the other gentle people
who are part of the fabric of my life.

PREFACE

The many changes in the Church and in the world in the past fifteen years raise the crucial question of how one makes authentic Christian decisions today. Life is more complex; there is a new emphasis on personal responsibility; and a new appreciation of the way God acts in the lives of each of his people.

This book is intended to help Christians who want to make decisions about their lives in compliance with the love of God moving within them. Such people can benefit from the process of discernment explained here in which one's personal history provides clues for making authentic life-decisions. Since the appropriation of one's own history in faith is the basis for this discernment, there are suggested exercises at the end of each chapter to introduce the reader into this activity.

I have chosen to focus the content of this book around the theme of making authentic decisions in the Lord. I *presume* that decision-making is not an isolated, few-times-in-a-life activity. I presume that the making of decisions is a constant in the reality of being human. Whether decisions are made less reflectively and more spontaneously or whether they are made after a great deal of reflection and prayer, life is specifically human because of the very ability to make decisions. Decision-making is the continuum of living whether it involves the time of rising in the morning or the choice of a new career. No human person exists without making decisions, and the making of decisions determines whether a person is less fully or more fully human. All the time-honored activities of loving God and neighbor involve decision-making. One becomes more fully Christian by "putting on the mind and heart of Christ" through authentic decisions in the Lord. Hence, though the focus of the book is the making of authentic decisions in the Lord, it is really dealing with the whole of spirituality.

Through this book, men and women who have made a personally directed, prolonged prayer experience may gain a heightened awareness of the historical as it became known to them in that experience. The book can also help them appreciate the presence of the consolation of their history in future prayer experiences. This applies in particular to the activity of contemplating in order to know and respond to God's love for them. While the exercises at the end of each chapter do introduce this activity, a more careful and deeper appropriation of one's history in faith will require special spiritual direction.

The book should be especially useful for spiritual directors who guide others through various forms of prolonged prayer experiences in which a decision in the Lord is to be made. At the end of each chapter a section on the "Role of the Director" gives a more detailed explanation of these phenomena and their significance, both for the director personally as well as for those they may direct.

After directing about 200 persons through the thirty-day experience of St. Ignatius' Spiritual Exercises and many more through eight-day prayer experiences I am deeply impressed by the significance of spiritual consolation for decision-making. "What is spiritual consolation?" and "How do you recognize it today?" are burning questions for a spiritual director. The further questions, "What is the significance of spiritual consolation for the decision-making process?" and "How is it to be used?", confront every director of prolonged prayer experiences.

Experience, study, and consultation have convinced me that one's personal history provides the locale for answers to these questions. This history, as more and more people are realizing, is the occasion and criterion of spiritual consolation. True spiritual consolation, of course, is a gift from God and the sign of his presence.

Every counsellor brings to his direction of others his own background and the tradition in which he was formed. Still, because the significance of one's personal history for growth in life is universal, I hope that my presentation of this topic—and in particular, of the importance of the consolation of one's history—will be helpful to all spiritual counsellors whatever their tradition.

Portions of the book are concerned with describing the experience of consolation and its significance in decision-making. Other sections have to do with definitions; still others with the experience of my own history or with the personal history of those I have directed. As indicated above, some suggestions concerning the role of a spiritual director are given, as are exercises to help in the different phases of appropriation. This word appropriation has here the meaning of a becoming aware of what it is to be a self, a making explicit of what has been implicit in one's consciousness.

In two or three places in the book where I describe my own history, it will be obvious how much I owe to others, especially my Jesuit confreres and companions in Christ. At the outset, I would like to express my gratitude to the Jesuit provincials who have supported me in the apostolate of spiritual direction. I have also shared these ideas to a great extent with the communities of Loyola House and Ignatius College in Guelph, and I have received encouragement and confirmation from them in abundance. Their patience with my importunities and their unfailingly generous and helpful response fills me with gratitude.

The significance of two communal experiences initiated by John LeSarge, S.J., when he was rector of Ignatius College is present in the book, especially in Chapter 10. The first of these communal activities was an eight-day retreat in which we prayed over our sin history and blest history as members of this community. The second was a four-week attempt at theological reflection upon our apostolate. The significance of our spiritual history (personal and communal) was dominant in both of these communal activities.

I am grateful to these Jesuits in particular: Fathers Joseph McArdle, Roger Greenwood, and John Veltri of Ignatius College, Guelph; Father Tom Walsh of Loyola Residence, New York; Fathers John Wickham and Keith Langstaff of Loyola

College, Montreal. These Jesuits have encouraged me greatly and offered positive criticism to my thought and writing. Roger Greenwood especially has spent many weeks with me trying to ferret out my thoughts and help me express them clearly.

I also received much support from Sister Susan Breckel, R.S.M. and Father John Malecki of Psychological Counselling Services, Albany, N.Y., for which I am most grateful.

The School Sisters of Notre Dame, St. Louis, Mo., deserve my special thanks for their willingness to listen to my thoughts on the appropriation of one's history. They prayed through the exercises I composed and shared their findings with me in a week long experience in the spring of 1977.

I would also like to thank Mrs. Pat Cottenie who patiently typed the many renditions of the book.

1 THE NEED FOR CHRISTIAN DECISION-MAKING

"And I said to you: Do not take fright, do not be afraid of them. Yahweh your God goes in front of you and will be fighting on your side as you saw him fight for you in Egypt. In the wilderness, too, you saw him: how Yahweh carried you, as a man carries his child, all along the road you traveled on the way to this place. But for all this, you put no faith in Yahweh your God, who had gone in front of you on the journey to find you a camping ground, by night in the fire to light your path, by day in the cloud." (Dt. 1:29-33)

There are three modern phenomena which can have great importance in Christian decision-making. The three I have in mind are these: the new sensitivity to interior spiritual activity, the growing sense of the importance of the historical in personal matters, and in an impersonal world, the felt need to make wise personal decisions. These phenomena deeply influence a prolonged prayer experience of Christian decision-making; and, alternatively, such an experience is significant for a person's sensitivity to interior spiritual activity, for consciousness of the importance of the historical, and for making personal decisions. I say a "prolonged" prayer experience to indicate that normally a deep influence will require many days, that is, ten to thirty.

In the last few years, I have become conscious of a new awareness of the spiritual elements of life on the part of many people. This is a fresh awareness of the spiritual movements within oneself rather than of one's practices of devotion or of external ritualistic acts. I find this new awareness in myself, and in many persons whom I have guided through a prolonged prayer experience. It also permeates much of the current and best spiritual literature. In fact, it is affecting the lives of all believing Christians.

This new awareness of interior spiritual movements is accompanied by an enhanced sense of the unique history each person experiences and desires to discover in our present day attitude to life in general. Thus it is to be expected that modern persons will seek to find a relationship between the interior experience of spiritual movements and their own history. They know history is an important element in understanding their situation. This is true in the theory and practice of psychology, sociology, and political science as well as that of history itself. A knowledge of one's past—whether ancestral, national, biological, or psychological—is considered basic for understanding the situation and the state of persons at any given time. Through different kinds of memory exercises people are finding ways to appropriate their own history. Since the faith is experienced in this atmosphere of historical consciousness, the appropriation of one's history in faith fits this recent dimension of human beings.

A further dimension in modern life is the need to make authentic decisions. A good decision has elements of the personal, social and divine. But it is the person's own decision. Such decisions emerge from the uniquely personal experiences of the individual, and spread out to benefit the society of persons far beyond the individual. We are finding that the new sensitivity to spiritual movements and the appropriation of our own history help us to make authentic decisions.

Decisions are authentic when they are fully personal, deeply felt, and free. These decisions come out of a fully human response to a situation. They respond to the many claims made upon a person—the cry of the poor, the ignorant and the suffering; the sense of one's inadequacy to meet the challenge; the awareness of evil and deception in one's own past as well as in a community's past decisions; the realization that the decision must fulfill a communal or public need, and that it is dependent for its validity on the community's acceptance.

Within the Roman Catholic community the issue of interiorizing the Christian faith in terms of the modern awareness of oneself as an evolving, developing person was crystallized by the Second Vatican Council. Alongside this new acceptance of oneself as an historical (existential) person, there is a constant awareness that decisions must be made within an ever-changing frame of reference and in the light of an unyielding faith in Christ. "Jesus Christ is the same today as he was yesterday and he will be for ever". (Heb. 13:8) The practice of presenting guidelines in terms of Christ's attitude for making decisions in the constantly unique situation of the believer indicates a new respect for the individual conscience.

Since John XXIII called the Second Vatican Council, Catholics have grown more aware of the challenges both of interiorizing their faith and of making authentic Christian decisions. Many changes have taken place in the liturgy, in moral issues, in church government, in the renewal of religious orders, in communications with other Christian churches and other religions, and in the Church's co-operation with all persons of good will, even with professed atheists, in order to build a better world. But the greatest changes are in the area of the spiritual life and its relationship to authentic Christian decision-making. This is equally true of the manner, the matter, and the context of our decisions.

In the past, decision making was mostly limited to obeying a series of laws passed down from a higher authority or to deducing specific obligations from general principles. Now much of this approach is gone. A body of moral doctrine is developing in the believing community. Yet, the application of this doctrine to our daily life is left to ourselves as we realize, more than ever, that we each have to discover our own unique way of coming to a decision while remaining within the larger faith-context of the believing community. We are encouraged to pray earnestly to God for light and discernment. The uniqueness of each one of us and of each situation is acknowledged as very significant to the manner in which we decide to decide.

The present world situation aggravates the difficulty of harmonizing the aspects of authority and responsibility in the

Christian vocation. While elements such as the worship of God in the Eucharistic celebration each Sunday, a life of marital fidelity, a life of prayer, a life of truth and justice, and concern for the poor and alienated remain, still many large and small decisions, as well as the myriad issues of everyday, have to be left to each one of us. We feel the need to know and follow the lead of the Holy Spirit in all of these.

The openness to other Christian communities, other religions, and other cultures is significant, for it indicates a plurality of approaches to any given issue. A Roman Catholic living in today's world of mass communications is bombarded by this plurality of religions, lifestyles, philosophies of life, and approaches to decision-making. We need a method for authentic Christian decision.

What makes this even more complex is the new spiritual challenge we are experiencing. We realize that our vocation is most sublime; in our heart is the secret of life itself—"I am loved beyond all expectation". We feel the urge to be the instrument of this truth by word and by lifestyle to other men and women so that they can participate in this love.

These two facts—experiencing God's love in our heart, and witnessing to this love in deeds—are not easily harmonized. The double and often difficult aspect of this vocation can be expressed in different ways. The Christian is to be in the world but not of it (Jn. 17:15-18). The person is to be a contemplative without neglecting action (Lk. 10-41,42). We are at once to love an unbelieving world and to bring to it the truth of Christ (Jn. 3:16; Lk. 6:27-35); we are to cooperate with all persons of good will in building a more human world; we are to relate in willing obedience to an authority structure within the believing community of the Church (Jn. 20:21,23). We are to follow our own conscience and the inspirations of the Holy Spirit that are uniquely our own.

In the past the areas of most of our decisions was limited to immediate family and parish. As Catholics, we felt that such decisions were made for us, if we remained within the womb of the Church. Even the awareness of when and how we were sinning against church laws was a form of security. From the cradle to the grave we knew what to do. Minute instructions were given even for our daily routine. Now all this has changed. The Church is no longer ahead of me but evolving with me. Today the believing community expects persons to be concerned about civic questions, world poverty and injustice.

The challenge of responsibility in the world has become crucial. I have to face the need I feel to make Christian decisions which harmonize with my life and rise out of my sense of responsibility for the world. "Hence it is clear that men are not deterred by the Christian message from building up the world, or impelled to neglect the welfare of their fellows. They are, rather, more stringently bound to do these very things" (*Vatican II*, pg. 233). What is this responsibility? How am I to go about fulfilling it? These are questions for individuals and groups.

Yet, so often, deception and indecisiveness are experienced by the modern Christian who seeks these answers. I am quite conscious that I may get involved in my own subjective needs or be deceived by my own or another's ideology. Because persons have become more cautious in the 1970's than in the 1960's, prayer for light is popular and recognized as necessary. The biblical charism of the discernment of spirits is invoked to help discover and carry through a course of action. But the method needs more clarification and updating.

There have been many different responses to the dramatic and even traumatic changes in the last fifteen years. Some have been fearful, some full of joy; some defensive, some open; some cloistered, some active; some, even confrontatory. Yet through it all, there has come a renewed awareness that God the Father is loving and merciful; that Jesus Christ is present and encouraging; that the Holy Spirit is enlightening and strengthening.

The biblical admonition to know and test the spirits has gained new prominence in such a climate. This new sensitivity to spiritual movements within us is in some ways comparable to those experienced with zen, transcendental meditation, and free association of images in non-Christian religions and psychological practices. The description of interior movements and their interpretation has found a new audience. Often, there is a desire to perform certain spiritual activities and discuss their effects within oneself and others by means of directed retreats and the sharing of prayer experiences, desire which arises from the fascination found in the understanding of self through these different spiritual phenomena, and from the strength derived from sharing such experiences.

Various forms of spiritual exercises are being used to help us focus on this type of spiritual movement and enable us to make authentic decisions. We are urged to consider a matter for decision while experiencing an interior attraction to God, for example, love, joy, peace, trust, and to seek a confirmation of our decision by a further experience of that same attraction. All this involves a procedure of following the lead of the Holy Spirit while contemplating the mysteries of Christ's life and then interpreting one's interior experience. Emphasis is placed on our uniqueness as persons using this way and the uniqueness of our dialogue with God. The basic contention is that, when one is being actively drawn to God in love, joy, peace and trust, good decisions can be made. This contention is based on the instruction of Paul in Galatians: "What the Spirit brings is very different: love, joy, peace, patience, kindness, goodness, trustfulness, gentleness and self-control. . . . Since the Spirit is our life, let us be directed by the Spirit. We must stop being conceited, provocative and envious" (Ga. 5:22,25,26).

It is obvious, then, that "consolation," that is, the experience of being drawn into God's love, is vital in such exercises. Today, we are newly aware of a form of consolation that can help in the process of decision-making. It has to do with the uniqueness of an individual's history. It is the "consolation of my unique history".

"Consolation" is more than a good feeling or pleasant experience. Consolation has that special spiritual meaning of being drawn towards God in a love that knows and loves all beings in the ambit of this love. "Did not our hearts burn within us as he opened up the scriptures to us" (Lk. 24:32).

When I have appropriated my unique history in terms of

my Christian faith, I receive a new experience of spiritual consolation that serves me in my decision-making and action. Briefly, it is God-given awareness that my history is meaningful and an expression of God's loving presence with me. This sense of true spiritual consolation arises quite easily in a prolonged prayer experience. Therefore, an understanding of this consolation and of its significance in making decisions is important to us as we live in today's *milieu* of interiority and history. This applies in particular as we pray through such an experience, and it is significant to the one directing us.

Many years of directing persons of all ages through such prolonged prayer experiences have led me to the realization that, in one way or another, at one moment or another, the question of a person's unique history is extremely significant in the whole of one's spiritual life and in the on-going experiences of prayer.

More and more the issue resolves itself into the question of our personal value and our decisions in a world that seems to devalue individual persons and take away our power of unique decision-making.

Experiences, both my own personal experiences and those as a director, suggest that these two issues of personal value and decisions can be best met by a prayerful consideration of one's history. When interviewing retreatants about their prayer, it is not long before their past experience with parents, teachers, friends, or employers surfaces and becomes a significant element. The director cannot help noticing that the element of reality is entering into prayer.

This consolation that my life story is an expression of God's loving presence is important today because it uses my modern historical consciousness to identify me closely with my Christian roots. It personalizes my decisions, my actions, my social and Christian life. Moreover, this consolation carries with it the element of uniqueness; the continual need to make decisions requires a guide such as the consolation arising out of this consciousness. The role of the Holy Spirit in each situation is known by the felt trail of consolation given in my history. In the discernment of spirits over a decision, the consolation of my history, already experienced and known, is a touchstone for judging and acting.

Since the thesis behind this book is that "the appropriation of one's unique history in faith resulting in the discovery of the pervading hand of God is important for authentic Christian decisions in today's world", the following reflection over one's history may serve to introduce the book's approach.

EXERCISE

A spiritual approach to my history

I begin from the stance of faith. Jesus is the Lord of my whole life, past, present, and future. In company with Mary my mother, Peter, Magdalen, Paul, and especially with Jesus Risen, I enter the memory of my life. The following words from Scripture may encourage me to compose myself: "With so many witnesses in a great cloud on every side of us, we too, then, should throw off everything that hinders us, especially the sin that clings so easily, and keep running steadily in the race we have started. Let us not lose sight of Jesus, who leads us in our faith and brings it to perfection: for the sake of the joy which was still in the future, he endured the cross, disregarding the shamefulness of it, and from now on has taken his place at the right of God's throne" (Heb. 12:1-2).

I seek the grace to "know as I am known", to see myself as Jesus sees me. I ask the Lord to give me an intimate understanding of my life's history as it relates to him, "the same today as he was yesterday and as he will be for ever" (Heb. 13:8). I ask for the consolation of my unique history.

First, I begin by remembering. This remembering is an awareness of exterior events in my life and my interior reaction to them. My memory makes them present to me. I remember those that are meaningful to me, whether pleasant or painful; and those I cannot find meaning for but am still searching out. Some key experiences that have been traumatic may remain hidden, but there will be signs of such hidden experiences in other reminiscences. So I recall incidents in my childhood with parents, grandparents, relatives, and friends: "Then I am reminded of the sincere faith which you have; it came first to live in your grandmother Lois, and your mother Eunice, and I have no doubt that it is the same faith in you as well" (2 Tm. 1;5). Some memories I enjoy, others I fear and find hard to face. In recalling school, college, and work, I bring to mind meetings with men and women friends and acquaintances, and I think back over the larger experiences of church, community, nation and world.

But I remember within a faith perspective. These events are recalled with the aid of the Holy Spirit's action of remembering in me: "the Advocate the Holy Spirit, whom the Father will send in my name, will teach you everything and remind you of all I have said to you" (Jn. 14:26). Sometimes the remembering is of obviously religious events that are significant. At other times the remembering is a kind of peripheral thing: the presence of God is known off to the side of one's vision.

Second, I will search to discover a pattern in my life experiences. Is there some recurring theme, a pattern, a mode, in my life experiences? Do the external events and situations relate to interior experiences? Does my interior state correspond to the external events? Does it depend on social contacts with parents, friends, or acquaintances? Do I see a repetition of experiences, whether of childhood, adolescence, or adulthood? Are there physical or psychological or spiritual signs that recur? Is the path of joy, suffering, fear, courage, desire, or generosity, a familiar one? What order do I see both interiorly and exteriorly in my life experience? When and how has God—Jesus—been most present in these? With a faith perspective on all this, do I get glimmers of a life-relationship with God that includes all the events—external, internal, social, spiritual—of my life? What image of myself do I find in my relationship with the Trinity—a lost sheep, a prodigal son or daughter, another Mary contemplating, another Peter, another John, a little child?

Third, I will be receptive to a sense of being whole. This will come when the activities of remembering and searching keep recurring as I compare my life to the human experiences of Jesus as given in scripture. I will experience the meaningfulness of my life when I sense my external activity and internal feeling coming together in harmony and wholeness. I let the historical context of times, places, and activities; of family, friends, work, and church give me its meaning. I wait for the moment when I realize that my experiences of the faith go beyond those moments of formal prayer and the Eucharist. I discover that my whole life is a theology, a revelation (a theophany?), and that God has shown himself to me in the uniqueness of my life experiences. Where and when have I found this sense of union before? Is it now present to me? What is lacking? How will it return, but with a newness? Wholeness comes as I continue the activity of remembering, searching and experiencing being whole.

Fourth, I move to openness. In this movement, I realize that the remembering searching, and sensing wholeness in my past open me to the future. So I enter into this knowledge of my history differently. I relate to my history consciously. It is a means to meet my future decisions and actions. The reliving of my experience from this stance of willingness gives me a new kind of knowledge. I allow myself to see how God has led me in past actions to fulfill his designs for me. I realize anew that God is faithful to his promises, these promises I now see are contained in my very history. The Lord has fulfilled them in me in the most unexpected ways. I open myself to see that my experiences have a similarity with those of the prophets, of Jesus, of Paul, and of the other saints. The dynamic now has four elements, and in openness I return to remembering, searching, being whole.

The four phases for appropriating one's own history are important. The activity has spiritual as well as natural connotations. It is more than the immediate recall of a computer or a photographic memory. In seeking to appropriate my unique history, the faith context of the activity sheds its own light on the past.

More specific reflections will be given after each chapter to help you understand its import affectively and to lead you to the comprehensive consolation of your unique history. While these activities may give you the impression that you will work out by intellectual effort a kind of computerized pattern of your life with God, this will not happen, nor is it the purpose of these activities. They look very discursive, but the overall expected result is affective. They are to enable you to compare the consolation of your past history with your present state of consolation during a decision-making process.

As I have indicated already, this book is a product of the process of reflection on my own experience of my own life history and reflection on the experience of the life histories of those I have been working with. In order that you as a reader will be able to grow in the appropriation of your own life history in faith, you too will have to reflect upon your own experience. I would suggest that the very reading of the book even without the exercises will help you to do this provided that you look upon all the material of this book as a multi-faceted dialogue. First of all there is the dialogue with myself as author; then there will be the dialogue with your own experience to see whether the reflections that I am suggesting do in fact correspond with your own experience. Then there is the dialogue with the Lord who is present now with you as you are reading these words. Then there is the dialogue with the Lord's word at the beginning of every chapter and in the quotations throughout. I believe that it will only be in the process of these faith dialogues that the full import of this book will be appreciated.

2 MEDITATING ON MY HISTORY

He has let us know the mystery of his purpose, the hidden plan he so kindly made in Christ from the beginning to act upon when the times had run their course to the end: that he would bring everything together under Christ, as head, everything in the heavens and everything on earth. And it is in him that we were claimed as God's own, chosen from the beginning, under the predetermined plan of the one who guides all things as he decides by his own will; chosen to be, for his greater glory, the people who would put their hopes in Christ before he came. Now you too, in him, have heard the message of the truth and the good news of your salvation, and have believed it; and you too have been stamped with the seal of the Holy Spirit of the Promise, the pledge of our inheritance which brings freedom for those whom God has taken for his own, to make his glory praised. (Eph. 1:9-14)

The significance of one's own history is recognized today by counselors of all kinds. The healing of memories is an important activity in both a secular and sacred context. The memory is used to recall one's conscious and preconscious experiences of past actions in order to gain freedom from the past, and to perform free and better actions in the future.

In a faith context, much of this is dependent upon a healthy relationship with God. The healing of memories in faith begins with the truth that God is loving and forgiving. The result of the dynamic is a growing awareness of this truth in the person's interior life and exterior activity.

When the events of my personal life are recalled in terms

of the question: "What is God doing with me through all my personal history?", I am beginning the process of appropriating my history in faith. I am not recalling to be healed or to be a forgiving person. I am recalling in order to discover the life pattern God has with me. I seek this for its own meaningfulness and for future action. I pray in keeping with the Lord's words, "Ask and it will be given to you; search, and you will find" (Lk. 11:9).

The two methods of going about this activity of appropriating one's own unique history can be compared to meditative and contemplative forms of prayer. The meditative style tends to be more discursive, with more mental activity than does the contemplative. In meditating more questioning and searching goes on and the knowledge and concern seems to focus more on myself in the God-myself issue than it does in contemplating.

This chapter will consider the meditative approach to appropriating one's unique history in faith. Chapter 4 will consider the contemplative approach. The two are quite different although they cover the same matter and often interweave with each other.

I will begin with a quite personal account to demonstrate what I mean by the appropriation in faith of one's unique history, as I discovered it in my own life of prayer. What leads us to investigate our own life's history in faith? How can we do this? What results can be hoped for? The examples from my own life may serve as introduction to the meditative style.

In recent years I have been forced by circumstances to ask many questions about myself and my relationship with others. This has eventually moved me to further questions: Why am I the way I am? Why am I so solitary? What is the significance of this solitariness? Why am I different from others? Why did I go to university? Why did I join the Jesuits? Why did I stay? What does this personal life of mine mean in the whole course of the world's events? Have I been a loving person? Have I moved the kingdom of Christ forward? What is the value of my life story? Does my history indicate the direction in which God is leading me? How can my history be an aid in my future life decisions?

Such questions must face the spirituality that John emphasizes. "God loved the world so much that he gave his only Son" (Jn. 3:16): and "this is the love I mean: not our love for God, but God's love for us when he sent his Son to be the sacrifice that takes our sins away" (1 Jn. 4:8-10). According to such a spirituality we should reflect constantly on the revealed fact that we are valuable in ourselves and not from what we do. Yet, seeking out the value of one's actions before God and other human beings does not seem to be a highly recommended spiritual attitude towards life. We are told we are in danger of reverting to pharisaism, scrupulosity, or guilt.

The existential question still arises, "Have we loved as Christ commanded us to?" We are faced with his words: "I give you a new commandment: love one another; just as I have loved you, you also must love one another" (Jn. 13:34). This question need not be asked to build up our ego, nor to attack it with guilt. It can be asked in grateful humility with a hope for the future. It can motivate us to reflect on the events of our lives in faith.

It is difficult for me to pinpoint when this need to discover the value and significance of my history became vital to me. I knew in faith that I was valuable. Yet, I had not been specifically instructed how to appreciate the historical aspect of my being. Possibly, the statements of Vatican II, with its existential, historical emphasis, encouraged me to reflect on the significance of my history as "revealing" the past and prophetic for the future.

The 1960's were years when I was scrambling with many different impressions. This was a time when I was completing my Jesuit studies and being ordained a priest. It was the time of tertianship, a year of growthful contemplation in a monastic setting in North Wales. It was a time of teaching college theology. It was the time I was master of novices after the Vatican II shakeup and the Jesuits' attempt at renewal and adaptation according to their 31st General Congregation. One kind of setting—studies, tertianship, novitiate—was filled with the old securities of the Church. The other setting—college theology, Vatican II, instructions for novices from the congregation—was filled with uncertainties and insecurities.

The 1960's were also a time of crisis in faith. Thinking back on my early faith I know that in the 1930's I was aware as a Catholic that the Church was presenting a different doctrine and life-style to me than my Protestant and non-believing friends were receiving. Later, in the 1940's at the state university, I realized Catholics did not exactly fit into the philosophy of education that governed it. The intelligentia of the university were dedicated to the method of the natural sciences. But the Church was solid and fulfilled a deeper need than the mechanistic, positivistic philosophy which governed the university. The mass, the sacrament of confession, and the presence of an unchanging community of faith, dedicated to avoiding mortal sin and preparing for death, surrounded me and gave me religious conviction. Even in religious life, it was a time when the "dry" sacramental life was the vogue. Everything was laid on from outside. One felt that acceptance there was determined by external practices in the novitiate, by examinations in intellectual studies, and by minute external requirements in the later years of formation. A person's interior life was supposed to be all-important, yet there was little encouragement to articulate and discuss it. Little was said about personal religious experience. As I relive these experiences I realize there was much anger in me at the time. Now, my feelings are of sadness that the affective life of the Church was not more fully engendered, and there is also a sense of amazement filled with joy that I do have a spiritually affective life.

By the late 1950's and early 1960's, this kind of dry faith life no longer seemed adequate. In fact, my own experience and that of many others, both within religious life and outside it, was to question the very existence of the soul, of mortal sin against God, and of the reality of the Church's sacramental life. Maybe this was because the efficacy of the sacraments was not externally manifest. Catholics appeared no better nor more dedicated than other people. Maybe it was because the triumph of technology and of marxism in China was forcing us to consider whether the only truth was that which could be measured in the science lab—pure materialism. Maybe it was fatigue from the stress of living in a Catholic ghetto, as the communication systems stormed its walls and entered right into the living room.

Vatican II seemed to be addressing itself to these questions with a kind of *apologia* for the faith and against a background of assurance that the Church was with mankind in its constant attempt to improve the state of human living. At the time of Vatican II, I was teaching college theology. Its documents were great material for my lectures. They gave that intellectual support the faith needed. But they did not give the faith! They did not quite supply for the doubts about the existence of the soul, mortal sin, the efficacy of the sacraments to improve life. The liturgical reform and the new openness to the world took away the old family (ghetto?) experience with its incense and mystery. I was confronted by the Vatican II challenge to become part of the world's forward movement. This was to be an expression of my faith. But what faith? The challenge forced me back to my roots. Could new shoots come forth?

The answer was to come in many different forms—cursillos, shared prayer, group dynamics, charismatic renewal, directed retreat experiences. All these were basically structured to assist people to have a religious experience and thus return or rediscover the faith they had grown up with. The emphasis was to be on experience, reflection on experience, and the validity of experience. This seems to have been my position along with others in the 1960's, I was searching through prayer and religious experience for the grounding of my faith.

But the exuberance of religious experience was only partially satisfying. Further questions about myself, my continued sinfulness, my indecisiveness, my relationship to the culture (scientific and historical), the Church and the world had to be met. True, with the confirmation and energy from religious experience, these questions within me could now be faced more directly. Vatican II, the bible, and the liturgy now became an aid in this personal search. As St. Ambrose remarks in *The Mysteries*, "the light diffused by the mysteries will penetrate more deeply into you than if explanation had preceded experience."

By the end of the 1960's I began to ask more particular questions concerning the directional aspect in my history. What had been taking place in the life of the Church and in my own life? Where was the Trinity in my life? What were They doing with my life?

These are fearful questions. Indeed, I could only begin to face them when my emotional life was in a crisis situation. At that time I experienced, imagined or real, a severe state of alienation. I thought that all I had been attempting to do was criticized or rejected by my friends to the extent that I feared greatly for my vocation as a Jesuit. Along with this came the sense of insecurity and unknowing that accompanies change and movement into the unknown. I experienced a great need for love and approval. Thanks be to God, this was given to me by many friends. On a retreat in 1972, the Lord also manifested his love for me in an extraordinary, deeply affectionate way. Since 1972, the continued development of the apostolate of spiritual direction at Guelph and the approval of superiors and fellow Jesuits have given further confirmation that there is value in my history.

The questions about my life now took this form.

> What does my history say about my ongoing life with God?
>
> What is the style, or mode, or pattern of the Trinity's unique relationship with me?
>
> How do they carry on their love-affair with me?
>
> What is the significance of the style and pattern of my past history for the future?

I see now that the questions are important because they point to the consolation from historical insight rather than from that of a fulfilled emotion.

In considering in retrospect when and how the value and significance of my life story became important for me, I am already reflecting on my history. I am aware that such needs are interspersed with the psychological and sociological conditions of the time. I realize that other needs also operate. Difficulties with the faith, the need for love and approval are all present. The issue becomes complex because these needs merge with and are part of the very history which I am trying to evaluate.

I realize now that there was much desolation, that is, anxiety and doubt, about my history and its significance to anyone, let alone my own injured ego. However, I persisted, off and on, in some kind of a state of gratitude and faith. I suppose the main grace I was seeking was the consolation of the Lord's continual love for me throughout my life. Now, I perceive that the desire for light in my darkness was part of the 'angst': "There must be something in my personal history that reveals God's style and mode of love for me!" So there was much investigating, examining, and questioning of my life in relation to God. The method was meditative and reflective.

Remembering

I started my investigation by recalling the more important incidents in my life and gradually became aware of things I had not thought about since the time of their occurrence. I can say that this activity was done in a context of faith and hope. It was like an extended examination of conscience. Later it became more meditative and eventually contemplative.

I see that my procedure was like an ever-expanding series of circles. Initially, I was caught up in the origins of my 'angst' and, therefore, in the most recent events of my history. Then I began to seek answers further back in my history, through the 1960's, 1950's, 1940's, 1930's, and even into the history of my parents and grandparents. These investigations were done at different levels of my memory. One level of recall was quite factual and objective; another was filled with interpersonal and emotional experiences. A third level contained spiritually affective experiences of faith, love, hope or doubt, mistrust, distance from God. On each level I was filled more and more with questions about God's leading me through my history, and about the style or pattern of relationship God has with me. At each level there was something insightful and wholesome, something filled with hope for the future. From the plateau of peace and quiet given to me by the Lord in the 1972 retreat experience, I began to look backwards with new spiritual awareness, and since 1972 this activity of appropriating my history has become more and more fulfilling.

What I refer to as the recall of factual matter can be divided into persons, times, places, activities. So with persons I recall my immediate family, my grandparents, close relatives, school friends, other friends, Jesuit confreres. In my own life the time periods tend to be broken up into the places I lived and the activities I was doing. From 1930-35, my earliest memories are of Dubuc, Saskatchewan; 1935-39, a change of village to Melville, Saskatchewan; 1939-44, two other changes of villages during the war years; 1944-45, my years in the armed forces; 1945-49, after the war and before joining the Jesuits; 1949-63, years of Jesuit formation; 1963-69, the years of apostolic work; 1969-72, the years of emotional and spiritual crisis; 1972-76, the years since the retreat experience in 1972. I recall also houses and places I have lived in, villages, towns, cities, farms, army camps, when I was in grade school, university, armed forces, working as a professional engineer, in the Jesuits. As I do this recall the above three—persons, times and places—become mixed in with activity. The summers in 1935-39 on my grandparents' farm on the Canadian prairies are very much present. I also recall my school years, laboring on farms and in warehouses, life in the army, studying, teaching, giving spiritual direction.

The reader will easily understand how the above recall leads into the more emotional recollections of interpersonal activity with parents, grandparents, school chums, girl friends, army buddies, university professors, work companions, Jesuit confreres, students, men and women religious, married couples. I remember moments of embarrassment with my parents, teachers and school friends—the time I lied about a little girl out of spite, the time I fought to save face with my school chums but was always unwilling to fight again. I remember the close friendship with my father, the impact of my grandmother on the development of my music and education. I remember the difficulty I had in making friends with the frequent moving, yet I found one or two kindred souls outside the university setting. Before entering the Jesuits I experienced an inability to establish a lasting relationship with two or three girls for one reason or another; this was both in my adolescent years and later when searching out a permanent companion for life.

My first sense of religious things came quite late in life. At eleven and twelve years of age I was introduced to the Catholic religion and the significance of the mass, communion and confession. My father was drinking heavily at the time and I was in a strange town. I took to these religious acts quite enthusiastically. Then, for some years during my life I was quite mediocre about the religious aspect of my life, although, there was some consistency about mass and confession. This continued through my years in the army. After the war, a new sense of religious values began with some acts of devotion. The good example of my aunt and uncle at this time was inspiring to me. This was the time of vocation questioning. In 1949, I entered the Jesuits and a totally new understanding of the Christian life and its significance for mankind was awakened in me.

Four intimate religious experiences are next recalled quite naturally. The first was when I was fifteen years old, the second when I was twenty-five; the third at thirty-nine; the fourth at forty-eight.

At fifteen I had a deep experience of Jesus' suffering on the cross while making the Stations during Lent. I recall that at this time the experience of my father's drinking habits and his preoccupation with money problems in the 1930's was quite a burden on me. I could not understand why my father acted as he did and suffered so much.

At twenty-five I made a kind of full surrender of myself to God. This was a time when I was suffering deep humiliation at my inability to do well in my engineering profession. For many years I had a nagging feeling that God was calling me to the priesthood. I tended to interpret the failures in my life as signs from God that I should surrender to his wishes. But the experience of call and presence in 1949 was much more than just a fatalistic reaction to the experience of inadequacy.

At thirty-nine in North Wales, I made the year of intense prayer, known as tertianship, at the end of my Jesuit studies. During the thirty-day Exercises of St. Ignatius, I experienced a deep conviction that God was a lover, a merciful and forgiving Father. I realized that God accepts me as I am, regardless of the success-failure standard of the world about me. I also grasped that I could rely on God's mercy for my salvation and not on my own actions. I became aware of the falsity and futility of legalism, perfectionism, activism, pelagianism, or whatever way one wishes to describe the false spirituality summed up in phrases such as, "I can save myself, if I only try hard enough." In my contemplations I experienced a sense of the reality of God's presence that I had previously thought limited to the saints. This was in contrast to the "dry" sacramental style of life I had been living in the 1950's. It was a time of interior personal religious experience not laid-on from outside. I was given a sense of personal worth that was not dependent on norms of success and failure. This whole year was filled with renewed hope and the desire to build Christ's kingdom.

Prior to this experience in tertianship, I had been very conscious of my inability to grasp musically, athletically, intellectually, and spiritually what I was reaching for. Still, positions of responsibility were being given to me and some success was to come in teaching and other activities. My biggest surprise came when it was suggested by one of my professors that I should teach college theology after completing tertianship.

In 1972, when I was forty-eight—at the end of a year of peaceful but fulfilling experiences writing a book and living with Jean Vanier's community of L'Arche in France—I made the retreat I have mentioned, I sought from the Lord some awareness of the value and significance of my history. At one point in my contemplations the Lord gave me an intimate understanding of his presence and love for me. By this experience I began to be affirmed in my desire to investigate my own history as part of the mystery of Jesus. I now felt drawn to contemplate the mystery of my own life as well as the mysteries of Christ's life. I realized the double action of contemplating the mystery of life as that of Christ's and my own.

Searching

This deep experience of the Lord's consolation had been preceded, as I have said, by some years of frustration, alienation, and even spiritual fear that I might reject my Jesuit vocation. The obligation of teaching theology in a college atmosphere threw me back into the syndrome of inadequacy and fear in the face of challenge. As I look back now, I realize part of the problem came from my past experiences of failure in examinations and performances before my Jesuit brothers. Another part of the problem came from a sense of frustration with the academic way of teaching theology to those who had no faith experience to serve as a basis for theological explanations. Yet, exteriorly, my students and fellow professors considered I was doing a good job. For a number of years after this I was master of novices; I experienced a great sense of inadequacy as I tried to meet the challenges of Vatican II for renewal and adaptation. With the many mistakes that I made, I also felt alienated from many of my Jesuit brothers.

The 1972 experience encouraged me to take stock of the other religious experiences in my life, and to search out the pattern of God's personal communication with me. In this searching activity, it is important to remember another searching that had been taking place in a different way for some years.

My studies in salvation history (1958-65) had shown the importance of the discerning role of the prophets in the Old Testament. The Trinity has written in large letters its love acts for the human race in the Old and New Testaments and in the Church. This relationship is also mine, if I discern it. When I discern it I see my significance to the Church and mankind. Experiencing this truth sets me free to make decisions and to act with Christ. Over the years I have known that the life of Jesus Christ is significant for me personally, and for what I am to do. This significance has come in many ways and on many levels of awareness. Among these are my experiences of the faith and the impact of the present culture on me, as well as my theological studies and prayer.

There has been the experience of relating to the faith of my elders—parents, sisters, priests, the worshipping community. There have been the moments of worship, of "The Beyond" at mass, of the sacraments and personal prayer. There has been the sense of identity with the great heroes of the faith from the reading of their lives. There has been a deepening of insight into the message of Christ by meditating on the words of scripture.

Alongside these developments were the interior experiences of my insignificance in the larger affairs of the world. The technologists were informing me about the population explosion, the starving millions, the shortage of resources and the abuses of justice throughout the world.

The psychologists and sociologists were making me aware of how my interior being was formed unconsciously by relationships with parents, or by the culture at large. I realized that much of my feeling life was determined by false guilt complexes and that it was important for me to do some healthy introspection, analysis, and even demythologizing of my own life.

My study of theology had led me to ponder the significance of Jesus' manhood under the title of the Second Adam. This, in turn, gave me some appreciation of the role of mankind in building God's kingdom on earth. I was struck in particular with the role of man's freedom in this enterprise of God. The significance of Christ for me was then intellectual. His life, death, and resurrection indicated two basic things to me. First, that I was loved beyond all my expectations; second, that human beings (myself included) could triumph over evil and death. My faith affirmed me on this intellectual level of my being. So I can say that these academic studies had a positive influence on my faith.

I suspected that the larger patterns in the Old and New Testaments, and the Second Adam theme pointed to me personally. It was only after the 1972 experience that I began in earnest to investigate the events of my own personal history as being an occasion of revelation to me. Then I started to see that the four religious experiences mentioned above might be focal points for my search.

When I place these four times and experiences as well as the other spiritual dimensions of my life in line with the events coming upon me from parents, friends, teachers, living conditions, some sort of pattern and style begins to emerge. I can observe periods of much prayer with a sense of union with God and periods of little or no prayer and not communicating with God (times of isolation). In examining these two periods of time, I notice something quite unexpected. In short, I realize that beyond what I thought was only a reaction to success, was the self-centered versus the altruistic.

At first, I thought my periods of union with God were connected to my state of helplessness and failure, and those times of not speaking with God, to my periods of success and physical well-being. But on closer examination I discovered the outcome has to do with two ways of relating to other persons, the one altruistic and the other self-centered.

At the time of my experience while praying over Jesus' death on the cross at the age of fifteen, my own life was relatively successful in school, sport, music and friendship with boys and girls. My father's drinking habits were the center of my concern. I prayed much for him and in this sensed a union with Christ. Later, when my father had overcome his drinking problem and the family was in good financial conditions (I was about eighteen), I experienced a time of failure and loneliness for me. My prayer was quite self-centered. I felt isolated from God.

In the army, I seemed on top of myself and things in general. My spiritual life centered around confession and the fear of hell. Again, it was an experience of isolation from God.

While at university, I had a religious sense of union with God, although my life of studies, work, friends (men and women) could be judged a failure. After university I had a period of work, sport and social life that was quite successful but somewhat sensual. I felt isolated from God. Life was a meaningless and grasping affair.

The experience of discontent and inadequacy in my work as an engineer led to a crisis situation. About this time I was also finding a new relationship with the Church in an adult sodality. At twenty-five, I made that act of surrender to God and entered the religious life. There was much confusion and fear, yet strangely enough, a sense of union with God.

In the Jesuit novitiate another experience was of solitude and aloneness with God, yet peace. I experienced a confirmation of my decision and pronounced my vows. During Jesuit studies I look back now and see that my experience was basically that of hanging on. There was no place else to go. I had little in the way of deep religious experience. A dry, self-centered spirituality reigned in the midst of some apostolic success while teaching.

While in my final year of ascetical theology (tertianship) I re-experienced my novitiate conviction and a whole new approach to God. Later as a college teacher, there was some success in the apostolate, some failure, a sense of inferiority and inadequacy in academic matters, and a new sense of sin and crying out to God for the meaning of my life, especially as I remembered the meaningfulness of my ascetical year. During this time, from 1963-72, there was a vague sense of God working through me in spite of my interior feelings of alienation and failure.

As master of novices, a sense of inadequacy and lack of preparedness for the job forced me to study and to appreciate the spiritual life in a new way. This would not have happened if I had not been appointed to this post. Another incident closely connected to this new appreciation of the spiritual life was the fact that the retreat apostolates in our province were being carefully investigated. This opened our community to consider a new apostolic effort; the personally-directed thirty-day prayer experiences came into being. Of course, there were other elements present in the culture at the time, but the coming together of need, humiliations, and the creating of this new apostolate is interesting. Following the new adventure into the work of directing prolonged prayer experiences in 1969 and its success, there was a further sense of poverty of spiritual gifts, hypocrisy, sense of sin, loneliness, isolation from Jesus. With the 1972 experience, and the new sense of the Lord's presence in my life as a spiritual director and as an instructor in this type of apostolic work, encouraged me to begin the activity of remembering and searching.

Wholeness and Openness

In this activity of recalling and searching for the pattern of God's relationship with me, I see that there were moments of wholeness and openness that confirm my life's activity, although these were not recognized at the time. Maybe this is because I experienced my life as conflicting rather than as developing and challenging.

Before 1972, I experienced conflicts, sometimes partially resolved but usually building on to new conflicts. Some of them are intellectual problems about the faith and its external effectiveness for the world and culture at large; but most of them are on a psychological or spiritual level.

What I formerly would classify as conflict, I now consider the developmental aspect of my own history. This development is connected also with where I have lived, the persons and institutions with whom I have related. So I see how my outlook on life has been an expanding one in relationship to the expansion of my environmental situation. I spent eleven years in a hamlet of about 200 people, then moved to a town of about 4,000 people for four years, then returned to the hamlet for two years, then to a small city of about 8,000 people, then to a university campus in a city of about 50,000 people, then one and a half years of extended travel and activity throughout Canada in the armed forces, then to a university in a city of about 800,000 people, and eventually into the Jesuits with their universal, worldwide outlook on life. My travels in Europe, as a Jesuit, further widened my horizons.

During these changes in geography and living conditions life was a conflict to me. I experienced the conflict of living as a Roman Catholic in a Protestant setting, then the conflict between a faith-approach to life and a secularist-empiricist one in two state universities. I knew the sort of conflict that exists between the spiritual ideal of human life which I considered as my faith, and the pleasure-seeking, physical-dominated, pride-oriented life promoted in the armed forces. I faced the inability to see myself as an engineer meeting deeper challenges. A romantic, idealistic world view which resulted from the study of the classics, literature, history, philosophy and theology, seemed in conflict with my inability to bring it about in the real concrete situation.

Until I entered the Jesuits I saw no possibility of synthesis between the faith perspective given to me at age eleven and the secularistic, empiricist approach to life I was experiencing in school, university, army and work. I thought there was a synthesis in the Catholic position given to me in the Jesuits. I was told that the end of life was to be found in the significance of Jesus for myself personally, and for man's relationship to man. Technology, progress, history were to be seen as means. This was theory to me. In the concrete the problem now expressed itself in the making of decisions. How was I to overcome self-centeredness and be outgoing? Later, the very idealism of the saintly life and its call to generosity brought about a further crisis, the crisis of being sinful, unfaithful and unable to fulfill the high ideals set for me spiritually, as well as a growing awareness that the Church herself was not having much effect on the decision-making process of the leaders of the world. My state was one of not feeling approved by men or by Christ.

The 1972 experience told me that I am approved and valued by Christ. And for that matter, so is the Jesuit community, the world, and all cultures and histories. I came to realize that my life is not determined by some static criteria of perfection but is a growth in understanding and an accepting of my history and of all history. Now insight and understanding are possible within the conflict, or with the lack of control of persons and things. This is because the conflict and lack of control means I am experiencing myself spiritually as human, developing and historical. There is a further consolation when I see this as a re-experiencing of the historical pattern of my life with God. Then I know wholeness and openness.

Different conflicts can be observed here. In the external order of things there is the conflict of a technological, materialistic perspective of life versus the more transcendent one. In the psychological I notice the conflict between my sensual needs and my deeply personal desires. In the social field I am aware of the conflict of self-centeredness and the more desirable attitude of altruism. In the spiritual understanding of things I experience a conflict of relating to God statically rather than developmentally. With Jesus, I observe in myself the feeling of not being approved by him and my continual efforts for his approval.

This means that I tend to move in faith from the materialistic barrier with its sensual reaction and self-centeredness, from failure and inferiority and a static evaluation of myself caught up in sin and desolation to a transcendental perspective with a compassionate personal reaction and availability to others. Life with Jesus is known as developing and valuable. Sin is understood, forgiveness sought, and hope grows. There is a sense of wholeness and openness.

I realize now that the conviction of myself spiritually as historical and developing is connected to my appreciation for Jesus as Second Adam and head of the human race in his resurrected manhood. The sense of wholeness and openness experienced in the historical and developmental dimensions of my life is a result of the contemplative aspect of my life.

Certainly, before 1972 my practice of searching out the pattern of God's relationship to my life was generally a reflective, meditative, examining activity, although I did discover in my year of ascetical theology and while teaching theology and directing novices that contemplation was most helpful in grasping the truths of the faith in our hectic and anxious world. And contemplation became the basis for the apostolate of helping to develop spiritual directors. However, the significance of this type of prayer for the appropriation of my unique history began to impress itself on me after 1972.

Through the simple method of contemplating the mysteries of Christ's earthly life I discovered the experience of being present to the Risen Christ in his mysteries. Theologically, I know I am an adopted child of God (Rm. 8:16,17) and that my life is a continuation of the life of Jesus. Thus I have been able to contemplate the mysteries of Christ's earthly life as a paradigm of the mystery of my own life. Paul's words, "to do what I can to make up all that has still to be undergone by Christ for the sake of his body, the Church" (Col. 1:24), and Jesus' statement to the apostles after the Last Supper, "I am the vine, you are the branches" (Jn. 15:5) indicate to me that my life is part of his life. But it is not identical to his. He is the Lord of history whose mission is to be savior of the whole world. Yet, he is risen and is present to me and the community of the faithful participating in this mission: "For where two or three meet in my name, I shall be there with them" (Mt. 18:20). The manner of relating my own life to the mysteries of Christ's life is a way to verify the wholeness and openness that I realize is part of the experience of appropriating my history in faith. I understand anew the instructions, when contemplating, to reflect on myself that I may gain new understanding, strength, courage, humility, etc., about myself [114].

Since 1972, a further appreciation of contemplation has arisen from my desire to come to the love of God. In particular this awareness has deepened through the "Contemplation to Attain the Love of God" as given in the *Spiritual Exercises of St. Ignatius Loyola* [230-237]. (Where numbers are given in square brackets throughout this book, they always refer to the text of the Exercises.) This new appreciation can be styled as contemplating the mystery of my own life. It has not taken me away from contemplating the mysteries of Jesus' life but has given them a new significance. This contemplative approach to the mystery of my life has made it possible for me to experience my life-history positively. I am able to grasp it wholly and openly.

I begin in the belief that my past life is valuable and of significance to mankind. I appreciate the Lord's word: "In the wilderness too, you saw him: how Yahweh carried you, as a man carries his child, all along the road you travelled on the way to this place." (Dt. 1:31).

Moreover, the very uniqueness of my history is something

God himself puts into being when he creates me free. More than that, I sense in my being that there is continuity, a development of my personal life with God. It is not just a series of isolated moments when God saves me by forgiving me, or raises me up by inspiring me, after which he returns to his inaccessible abode in heaven. My unique history involves the continual personal presence of God with me through infancy, childhood, adolescence, adulthood, failures and triumphs, sins, transcending acts, desolations and consolations. The same mysteries of Christ's life—his conception, birth, adolescence, adulthood, failures, triumphs—are with me. Contemplating these elements of my own life in conjunction with these mysteries of Christ's life can lead me to find a sense of wholeness and openness.

Possibly, it is from the many repetitions of the "Contemplation to Attain the Love of God" that I have decided to consider the appropriation of my history in faith under the activities of remembering, searching, being whole and being open.

THE ROLE OF THE SPIRITUAL DIRECTOR

The following brief and sometimes obvious statements are intended to help you as a spiritual director come to more fully developed principles and skills in guiding others to meditate on their own history.

A. Readiness

Not all persons are ready to investigate the value of their life. But when the time is right they will be doing this somewhat naturally or will have a desire to do it.

B. Listening

As with all spiritual direction, listening is the most basic skill of the director. Listen carefully and with faith to the account of life that is being given. Listen to how it is being given.

C. Affirming

Support the personal worth of the one being directed. Be sensitive to those moments of value in the life that is being recounted before you.

D. Clarifying

By questions and suggestions help to bring understanding to the reflection on experience; sometimes laying the groundwork for the discovery of reasons for guilt feelings and inadequacies; sometimes facilitating the discovery of the positive elements in the person's life story.

E. Pointing out the activity of Jesus

After perceiving the consolations and desolations that exist in the personal history, and at the proper time, point out the activity of Jesus in this history; for example, you might suggest: "Consider all the spiritual benefit that others have gained through your presence, even though you were going through so much psychological pain at the time." You may also point out the false leads that come from desolation, often associated with compulsion, impatience, false guilt.

F. Objectifying

Help the person to see life more realistically. Keep showing the presence of Jesus in their personal history. You can help begin this investigation of the past, little by little, by examining carefully with the person what led up to the various experiences of consolation and what followed these.

G. Encouraging

Encourage the one being directed to keep taking the risk of loving others while seeking light about compulsive activity. The need to act opposite to this and other selfish traits is to be encouraged. As the person meditates past personal history there is usually a growth in the awareness of sinfulness, self-centeredness and limitations even as progress is made in loving. This awareness can throw a person into discouragement;

but once again, the question of the value of one's personal history will emerge. At this point the director will encourage a more insightful approach to meditating one's personal history all over again: "Perhaps you could once again meditate over all those events but this time look for and appreciate the very compassion, sympathy, patience and gentleness that has come from those events which contained failure and emotional pain."

EXERCISE

Getting in touch with my own life-questions

Introduction

Is not man's life on earth nothing more than pressed service, his time no better than hired drudgery? Like the slave, sighing for the shade, or the workman with no thought but his wages, months of delusion I have assigned to me, nothing for my own but nights of grief. . . .
What is man that you should make so much of him, subjecting him to your scrutiny, that morning after morning you should examine him and at every instant test him? Will you never take your eyes off me long enough for me to swallow my spittle? Suppose I have sinned, what have I done to you, you tireless watcher of mankind? Why do you choose me as your target? Why should I be a burden to you? Can you not tolerate my sin, nor overlook my fault? It will not be long before I lie in earth; then you will look for me, but I shall be no more. (Job 7:1-3, 17-21)

These were Job's life-questions. As he pursued his questions he became filled with hope: "I know that my redeemer lives" (Job 19:25). I too am filled with life-questions—questions unique to me, questions that have been with me for some years, some clearly enunciated, others basic to my struggle for growth.

Suggested Approaches

I pray for the grace of enlightenment and hope. I ask the

Risen Lord to help me meditate on my own history so that I may realize its value in his eyes and for all humanity.

I pray for light as I begin examining myself to find out what questions are present in my being about my existence, my failures, my successes, my journey through life, about the value of my life.

When and how did these questions arise? Was it at a time of deep religious experience, a time of crisis, fear, or the taste of wormwood after success, or a sense of aloneness?

What encouraged me to continue the investigation? Was it the experience of love from my parents and friends, wife and children?

Was it some peak religious experience that urged me to find the meaning in my own personal history?

Did I find any support for this type of prayer over my history when I read such passages in scripture as "Jesus increased in wisdom, in stature, and in favour with God and man" (Lk. 2:52)? Did the account of Jesus' temptations in the desert and in the Garden of Gethsemane help me?

As the Lord leads me, I will begin from the point of questioning or of hope or of desire and move forward or backward in my memory to seek out in the Lord the meaning and value of my life.

3 THE CONSOLATION OF MY UNIQUE HISTORY

Blessed be the God and Father of our Lord Jesus Christ, a gentle Father and the God of all consolation, who comforts us in all our sorrows, so that we can offer others in their sorrows, the consolation that we have received from God ourselves. Indeed, as the sufferings of Christ overflow to us, so, through Christ does our consolation overflow. When, we are made to suffer, it is for your consolation and salvation. When, instead, we are comforted, this should be a consolation to you, supporting you in patiently bearing the same sufferings as we bear. And our hope for you is confident, since we know that, sharing our sufferings, you will also share our consolations. (2 Co. 1:3-7)

The spiritual consolation of my unique history is significant for two reasons, and they are complementary. The first is its importance in the making of authentic decisions today. The second is the sense of reality and well-being it gives me for my daily spiritual life.

At certain times in one's life a person is aware of making responsible and authentic decisions in keeping with the faith. When such decisions are considered carefully, it is realized that they have been made out of love. With further reflection the significance of St. John's words may be appreciated: "My dear people, let us love one another since love comes from God and everyone who loves is begotten by God and knows God. Anyone who fails to love can never have known God, because God is love. . . . this is the love I mean: not our love for God, but God's love for us when he sent his Son to be the sacrifice that takes our sins away" (1 Jn. 4:7-10). Thus, responsible and authentic Christian decision-making is dependent upon a context of the love of God for us, a context that exists before, during, and after our decision and action.

Consolation and Decisions

This love of God that floods our hearts acts as a spiritual consolation to us in deciding and taking action; and this consolation is affectively experienced both as coming from God and returning to God, as being received and given back again. Consequently, Christian life requires an increased awareness of consolation for decision-making. A most important experience of God's love for us, always present but often not perceived, is the spiritual consolation I here describe as the consolation of one's unique history. It is the awareness of God's comprehensive and continual love for us as experienced throughout our life.

The activity of the Holy Spirit is the love of God moving us to love other persons, even our enemies (*cf.* Lk. 6:35). The discernment of interior movements or spirits is a process of judging whether the decision to which we feel interiorly moved is good or better than its contrary. We know the activity of the Holy Spirit by the state of true peace, goodwill, kindness, compassion, and hope, in our being (*cf.* Ga. 5:22).

The need for a decision usually occurs in a crisis, when, for instance, I am faced with a question or problem, when I feel angry or fearful of alienated; when basic needs clamor for fulfillment, when my expectations are disappointed, or when I stand in need of forgiveness. Whatever the nature of the crisis, what finally moves me to responsible and authentic Christian decision and action is the awareness that I am the passive recipient of God's love; this awareness is spiritual consolation. And when the decision is made spiritual consolation is the sign of correct decision, but now in the felt conviction that I am actively loving God in return (a further expression of grace!). In the spiritual activity of deciding and acting, I need the guidance of this consolation. The complexity of modern life, with its multitude of variables, requires an awareness of when I am actually experiencing God loving me, as well as the times when I am loving him in return.

This agrees with the thought of St. Ignatius Loyola. The main issue for him in the making of proper decisions is to know whether or not one is moved by the love of God and is experiencing true spiritual consolation. As Ignatius says: "The love that moves and causes one to choose must descend from above, that is, from the love of God" and "For just as in consolation the good spirit guides and counsels us, so in desolation the evil spirit guides and counsels. Following his counsels we can never find the way to a right decision" [184, 318].

The Historical and Decisions

Christians have always had to make personal decisions. In the past, however, there has been a fairly stable structure of life, both within and beyond the believing community, that made the outcome of even difficult deliberations fairly easy and predictable. Everyone believed that God's will was mediated, even in fine detail, by the Church. Now, it is not merely change that makes the task of decision-making more arduous but also the pace of change.

Furthermore, global communication has opened up a multitude of cultural approaches and a resultant plurality of possible decisions and solutions. As individuals, Christians are led to rely on a more immediate experience of the Holy Spirit inspiring and confirming them in their decision-making. They need a method of correctly discerning the meaning of their experience.

What is the importance of the historical for spirituality today? How is the historical of special significance in making authentic and responsible Christian decisions today? When the Church, in Vatican II, questioned her own significance, she did so by looking not merely within but also beyond herself. She needed more than one source of knowledge for discernment. The urgency of discerning the 'signs of the times' became one of her concerns. She discovered many signs; she recognized the signs of God's activity in the free spirit of mankind as well as the signs of man's enslavement. She admitted the relevance of the historical in today's world. The activity of appropriating my history in faith is an acknowledgement of this.

The decree on "The Church Today" indicates, for example, that the Church is historical and has developed along with mankind (*Vatican II*, pgs. 245-6). People are undergoing a more thorough development of their personalities (pg. 240) while growing more and more free (pgs. 262-3). Indeed, humankind is in a state of social and cultural transformation (pg. 202) that has changed its static concept of reality to a more dynamic and evolutionary one (pg. 204). Throughout this development and not just at the end, this human activity is valuable to God (pg. 232).

The Church sees that humankind is already approaching life in terms of history, and the Church desires to encourage us to appropriate our history in the context of faith rather than doing so independently of God (pg. 217). In this appropriation, it is necessary for us to recall that Jesus is the Lord of history (pg. 247) and that only in the mystery of Jesus does the mystery of ourselves take on light (pgs. 220, 222). Here the true value of our freedom is recognized (pg. 214).

Vatican II insists that work develops persons historically and carries them beyond themselves (pg. 233). Everything on earth is created for the human person (pg. 210) but, in the great ongoing social and cultural transformation (pg. 202), it is important to recognize the value of the historical movement towards social unity (pg. 241). In short, Vatican II has indicated that humanity cannot be understood apart from the historical, and that discerning the lead of the Spirit cannot be done apart from the historical.

The Consolation of My History

First, what is true spiritual consolation? It finds its expression in an increased or intensified sense of faith, hope, and love that I place in God. I know experientially that I am loved by God and that I am taken-up in the interchange of receiving and returning this love. With such love I know the goodness and faithfulness of God so that faith and hope well-up in me, and I find contentment, peace, and completion. It can also be when I feel caught up in God, a friend of Jesus, even embraced by Christ. St. Paul speaks about "the love of Christ overwhelms us" (2 Co. 5:14), "Caught up . . . right into the third heaven" (2 Co. 12:2), "trying to capture the prize for which Christ Jesus captured me" (Ph. 3:12), "this hope is not deceptive, because the love of God has been poured into our hearts by the Holy Spirit which has been given us" (Rm. 5:5).

The description of St. Ignatius Loyola is helpful at this point. He describes consolation in this way:

I call it consolation when an interior movement is aroused in the soul by which it is inflamed with love of its Creator and Lord, and as a consequence, can love no creature on the face of the earth for its own sake, but only in the Creator of them all. It is likewise consolation when one sheds tears that move to the love of God, whether it be because of sorrow for sins, or because of the sufferings of Christ our Lord, or for any other reason that is immediately directed to the praise and service of God. Finally, I call consolation every increase of faith, hope, and love, and all interior joy that invites and attracts to what is heavenly and to the salvation of one's soul by filling it with peace and quiet in its Creator and Lord [*316*].

Such a description of consolation will always be valid. Still, the appropriation of my history in faith adds a further dimension to this description that will help me recognize true spiritual consolation and use it in decision-making. Thus, a second question arises, "What is the consolation of my unique history?".

Rather than attempting a definition, I will describe it by the forms of awareness that characteristically accompany it. For example, I may become aware that I am valued; that I am sustained through life beyond any merits of my own as Paul says in Ephesians (*cf.* Eph. 2:1-10). I am aware of the value of my life's efforts as also given by God. I may have an intimate understanding of myself as an adopted child who shares in the work of the Son, Jesus, precisely as carried out in my everyday life. I know my life as a beloved sustained contingent existence; a beloved sustained development; a beloved sustained continuum of unique concrete incidents. I realize the whole of my history as having meaning because of God's presence in it, his loving in it, his association with me. My life is one constant expression of God's creative and redemptive love. In brief, I have a comprehensive awareness of myself and my whole life as loved with Christ. I experience myself in terms of God's unique love: "My delight is to be with the children of men" (*cf.* Prov. 8:31). I have a new consciousness of my history, an experience of its uniqueness, and a sense of God's comprehensive and continuous presence throughout my history.

The experience of God's continuous presence throughout my life has some similarity to the earthly life of Jesus, and his historical way of knowing true spiritual consolation. Jesus' humanity both before and after his resurrection is of great spiritual significance to me. As Second Adam and new head of the human race, Jesus' life's history is a paradigm for everyone. Just as his unique life's history was a consolation to him, so mine can be a consolation to me. The difference is that Jesus fully appropriated his history and knew its significance through prayer to his Father.

The point in praying over my history is to discover its uniqueness. True, the history of the human race is unique in the way that history never quite repeats itself. One might speak of the unique history of the people of this continent, this nation, this city, this family. But, my history is personal to me alone. I am not a mere number, even a cipher, in a computerized society. Its uniqueness lies in my spiritual relationship with God, the three persons in the Trinity. I pray over my history to gain an awareness of my own personal love-life with the Trinity which has been actualized in my history, even if not fully experienced or understood. This awareness can, and even should, lead me to the knowledge that God values me most especially—a knowledge so deep that its verification in me is an overwhelming humility. This concern for me is not only special in relation to others, but my own history is given me by God over all the possible histories that might have been mine. And this consolation is humbling in the most positive sense.

A further element in this consoling experience of praying over my unique history is the abiding presence of God. Such prayer gives me an awareness of God's faithfulness. He has been present to me throughout my history. I can become aware of the pattern of God's personal faithfulness to me in praying over my own unique history, an awareness that is much "sweeter than honey to my mouth" (Ps. 119:103). It is this sense of God's faithfulness that helps me appreciate the spiritual insights and discernments of the prophets, other spiritual giants, and even Jesus himself. Simply, they understood the significance of the historical in God's actions with themselves, with Israel and with the new Israel, the Church. Many biographies and spiritual journals, for example, those of Augustine, Teresa of Avila, Newman, and Merton, disclose this kind of awareness. When Ignatius says: "God treated me as a teacher instructs a child", he expresses an awareness of this special manner of faithfulness at certain times in his history. The increased appreciation of the lives of Jesus, of the prophets and of the saints that comes from praying over my own history may be considered a confirmation of this method.

The following (printed with permission) is a description of someone else's prayer that expresses in part the consolation of one's history:

Sometimes when I am praying, the Lord seems suddenly to invite me to come to a place of great peace and love where he is intimately present. In this experience, I know him differently from the ordinary way He relates to me in prayer. With no words, and no effort on my part, I am deeply aware of his love for me, in spite of all my unworthiness. There is intense joy, and contained in this joy, I have the vivid awareness of his forgiveness, of his complete understanding of everything about me, and above all, of the loving, almost playful relationship he wants me to have with him. All worry and anxiety are excluded from my mind. He fills my whole thought.

Since this experience usually happens when I am praying on the Passion or something connected with it, there is often the feeling of the defencelessness of Jesus in opening his heart to us so completely. Quite often I come close to tears in this prayer. In these thoughts, too, there is the strong certitude that it has always been so. In all my history, the Lord has offered me his faithful love. He was always calling me to this place of rest. He was always waiting for me to turn to him in this way.

After these prayer experiences, I am left with the strong impression of having been somehow invited to glimpse the mystery of God's friendship for sinful man.

Such a description of God's comprehensive and continual presence and friendship explains his full and continual entry into my own human condition, and into the human condition of all persons (Jn. 15:4). Paul says that we have all sinned in Adam (Rm. 5:12). Consequently, Jesus can enter into John's baptism for sinners because he is a member of the human race. In sin there is inevitably a social dimension spreading out in ever-widening circles, until all of the human race is included. We live in an interdependent world and are increasingly aware of the social effects of sin. All my activity, whether sinful, secular or sacred reaches out to touch my ancestors, my parents, my teachers, my friends, and my worlds of business, work, politics, nation, and church.

Spiritual consolation resulting from the appropriation of my history is of its very nature social and future-oriented. It carries with it the willingness and desire to meet the challenges of the present, challenges which arise both from within me and from everyone with whom I am in contact. The state of other people and their personal histories can equally constitute challenges to me. I live among others in this world and have to face the challenges presented by them, their needs, their demands, their personal and unique histories. Although the final basis for judging a situation and deciding on an action rests in the appropriation of my own history, that judgment and decision cannot but be influenced by the demands and histories of those around me. Indeed this would seem to be the way the Spirit is leading me to consolation today, by harmonizing my decision, which involves the demands and histories of others, with the appropriation of my own history.

In a Retreat Situation

The appropriation of my history with its accompanying consolation often happens during a prolonged prayer experience, such as the Spiritual Exercises. When this is so, such a prayer experience becomes an excellent instrument for responsible and authentic decision-making. In such an experience, many different exercises of prayer are used to help in recognizing true spiritual consolation so that decisions can be made with the Lord. The experience in prayer over my creaturehood and sinfulness which lead me to gratitude and sorrow before the abiding love of God, the experience of being with Christ by contemplating the mysteries of his earthly life which lead me to spiritual freedom, the experience of diverse spirits which lead me to discernment with the help of a spiritual director: all these help me to become open, and they give me an intimate knowledge of true spiritual consolation that I can use in making choices with the Lord.

The historical consciousness prominent in today's culture will exert its influence in the course of a prolonged prayer experience. In praying about my basic position with God, the sense of history can appear when I consider my "indifference" to a long or a short life. A proper understanding of my response to God's love already given to me can evoke an awareness that I am being continued in existence because of God's love.

History is a dominant consideration in praying over my sins. To recall the data of my sin history is a good introduction to experiencing my sinfulness in the face of God's goodness and mercy. Here is one way of going about it:

This is the record of my sins. I will call to mind all the sins of my life, reviewing year by year, and period by period. Three things will help me in this: First, to consider the place where I lived; secondly, my dealings with others; thirdly, the office I have held [56].

If the recall of my sin-history leads to a sense of sinfulness, I have received the grace I sought. In the interpersonal life with God that prayer presumes, my appreciation of God's fatherly love directly influences the intensity of my sorrow. I may begin to wonder at this kindness and mercy. I may begin to acknowledge historically my growth in grace. I may even discover a new kind of responsibility for all the growth dimensions in my life as I think more cosmically and historically.

If I am praying for an affective knowledge of the Lord's humanity then my prayer is concerned with knowledge of the historical Jesus. Contemplations on the Lord's life follow Jesus' history from childhood to adulthood in Nazareth, to his further growth as he meets suffering in the hard-heartedness of the scribes and pharisees.

In contemplation I ask to "love and follow him more closely" and then I reflect on myself to gain some benefit. To pray in this way over Jesus' life will often bring in events from my own life which become important elements of resolution to me. At this moment my own growth will be an important element in prayer. Prayer over Jesus' passion and resurrection extends and completes the historical treatment of Jesus' life.

When I wish to respond in love to God, the consideration of my own history is most important. To this end I am "to recall to mind the blessings of creation and redemption, and the special favors I have received" [234]. Whether the elements of my blest history are appreciated as historical and as developmental depends on me, but this is more likely to occur today when people have a more highly developed historical consciousness than in past generations.

Discernment and Decision

Since the thesis of this book is concerned with appropriating my unique history in faith and decision-making within and beyond the experience of a prolonged prayer experience, certain attitudes are therefore important. The consolation of my history should help me to be open to the future possibilities: "I should be like a balance at equilibrium, without leaning to either side, that I might be ready to follow whatever I perceive is more for the glory and praise of God" [179]. Indeed, the appropriation of my history ought to give me a more sensitive awareness of the love that is to motivate me: "The love that moves and causes one to choose must descend from above, that is, from the love of God" [184]. Similarly, the experience of this consolation will help me to judge the decision in ultimate terms: "This is to consider what procedure and norm of action I would wish to have followed in making the present choice if I were at the moment of death" [186]. By this time I have reached the point of decision-making in a prolonged, directed prayer experience. I should be discerning in terms of the comprehensive consolation coming from my own history. The more I have appropriated my history in faith, the more I can judge and be motivated correctly by this consolation.

The activity of appropriating my history is important for discernment on two levels: the existential (Where has the Lord been present?) and the rational (How has he been present?). Both of these levels, of course, unite in me. This can occur at the very beginning of a retreat when I ask myself the question: "What ought I to do for Christ?" The question presumes that I know what Christ has been doing for me and that I am in touch with the love act of Jesus on the cross as it reaches down the centuries to me and penetrates all my personal history. This presumption suggests that the knowledge of what and how Christ has been in my life is important for discernment both on the rational level, where I know with my head, and on the existential level, where I know with my heart. These levels will be most apparent when the sense of harmony is experienced.

By the activity of appropriating my history in faith I dispose myself to receive this spiritual consolation, since the consolation of my history is a grace to be sought from the Lord. It is not something I can achieve by self-examination only. The dynamic interchange presumed in any grace-filled experience is also presumed here. The grace in question is the realization of God's presence throughout my history and the pattern of my relationship with him. I am asking to know both rationally and affectively this grace as it comes to me from God. I dispose myself for this grace by engaging in the four phases of remembering, searching, being whole, and being open.

A specific consolation attends each of the phases of appropriation. In each phase the consolation is a grace which is independent of my activity, although concomitant with it. When I am remembering, I may have the sense that I am in fact entering into Jesus' memory of my life. In searching I may be exhilarated to discover in my life a pattern similar to that in the life of Jesus. In the third phase I may sense a wholeness resulting from the deepening union of my life with the life of Jesus.

In the fourth phase my sense of openness to the forward direction of my life may be experienced as union with Christ in his own openness to the paschal mystery. These specific consolations converge to form the comprehensive consolation attendant upon the complete appropriation of my history in faith.

The appropriation of my unique history in faith is both an action and a result of action. It is never complete. It is living. It is concerned with my history. It is an activity by which I seek to understand the meaning of my life in reflecting on my history in a faith context. It is a reflection on my past as I recall it, not in terms of psychological or financial or social states only, but in a faith perspective. This means that I am reflecting on my life in terms of mysteries of Christ's life and as it has been lived in the ambit of God's abiding presence. This history is personal and unique. Although others may know certain features of my history, even a great deal, no one really knows it completely but God. It is unique because it concerns the interpersonal relationships that I have with God and others.

To engage in discernment means that I wish to follow the lead of the Spirit as present in my history. Therefore, I seek to know the forward direction of my history in order to use it for correct decisions regarding the present and the future. I first recall the more obvious signs of the Lord's presence in my life and then start to investigate and search out the unique way in which the Lord has been present with me.

I may only begin appropriating my history at the end of a directed, prolonged prayer experience. If this happens, I will come to realize that the directives for decision-making will be different outside such an experience than they are during the course of it. Moreover, I may gain the insight that directed prayer experiences are intended to meet me where I am and then help me to grow.

THE ROLE OF THE SPIRITUAL DIRECTOR

The following comments are intended to help a spiritual director come to more fully developed principles in guiding others to the consolation of their personal history.

A. God's gift

The director should always be aware that what is being sought is not just a natural insight but rather is a consolation, a gift from the Lord, a gift above and beyond the sheer investigation of one's unique history. The fact that the one being directed has sought help in this process indicates that the meditation over one's history has begun.

B. Locating influential moments

The director helps the person to locate the turning points in his or her life history. Later the activity of moving forward and backward from these turning points, or influential moments should be encouraged. By means of questions, the one being directed can be led to consciousness of the continual presence of God throughout the series of events that otherwise would seem to have no connection. The director encourages the person to appreciate the mystery of these events.

C. Pointing out paradoxes

Often the director will be able to perceive well in advance the expressions of paradox in the other person's life history. For example, the director may perceive where external failure has led to spiritual union with God, or where weakness has been the occasion of interior strength, or a mistake has opened a whole course of action that is led by the Spirit. These the director will point out when the person is ready to appreciate them.

EXERCISE

To appreciate my history as a unique experience with God

Introduction

Thomas, called the Twin, who was one of the Twelve, was not with them when Jesus came. When the disciples said, "We have seen the Lord," he answered, "Unless I see the holes that the nails made in his hands and can put my finger into the holes they made, and unless I can put my hand into his side, I refuse to believe." Eight days later the disciples were in the house again and Thomas was with them. The doors were closed, but Jesus came in and stood among them. "Peace be with you," he said. Then he spoke to Thomas, "Put your finger here; look, here are my hands. Give me your hand; put it into my side. Doubt no longer but believe." Thomas replied, "My Lord and my God!" Jesus said to him: "You believe because you can see me. Happy are those who have not seen and yet believe." (Jn. 20:24-29)

Thomas was filled with the consolation that in fact Jesus was very much alive. He had been continuously present with Thomas during this week of doubt. Jesus has also been with me in my history of doubts, anger, sins, failures, successes.

Suggested Approaches

I pray that I will be filled with a deep-felt awareness of God's continuing presence in my personal history and of myself as a continuing, evolving, developing person who has constantly participated in God's unique love-act for me.

I ask the Lord to give me light as I reflect upon my life. Do I see spiritual incidents that began a long series of connected events? Were these incidents expected: Were they something I foresaw because of the place in which I was living, my family, school, work, religion? I ask to recognize when the affective element with God was present. Where did this happen? How was I conscious of God and the sense that he had been with me throughout these events?

I keep seeking in the Lord by considering if these initial moments were unexpected. Were they the result of an accident, a financial crash, an unexpected success? Were they initiated by some outside influence in the home, at school, or in business? Did they begin with some unusual interior reaction to circumstances? That is, was there some uncontrolled emotional response, such as anger or love, that moved me? Was there a spiritually emotional experience of conversion, sorrow, fright, longing for God?

4 CONTEMPLATING MY HISTORY

It was you who created my inmost self
and put me together in my mother's womb;
for all these mysteries I thank you:
for the wonder of myself, for the wonder of your works.

You know me through and through,
from having watched my bones take shape
when I was being formed in secret,
knitted together in the limbo of the womb.

You had scrutinized my every action,
all were recorded in your book,
my days listed and determined,
even before the first of them occurred.

God, how hard it is to grasp your thoughts!
How impossible to count them!
I could no more count them than I could the sand,
and suppose I could, you would still be with me.

(Ps. 139:13-18)

Where the second chapter was concerned with meditation on our own life events, this chapter will deal with the function of contemplation in appropriating one's history. This involves contemplating the mysteries of Christ's life in conjunction with one's history and in the direct contemplation of the mystery of one's own life. As mentioned in the first chapter, the process of contemplating is less discursive than that of meditation since it is more passive and more oriented to mystery. Here again, I will include personal data to explain the method, and I will refer to a special method of contemplating that leads one to seek and find God in all things. In this way questions and answers such as these will develop:

1. How does the experience of contemplation enhance the experience of appropriating one's history? It heightens the sense of God's presence throughout one's life.
2. How does the experience of appropriation affect the experience of contemplation? It gives the aspect of reality to one's contemplating.
3. How does the method of contemplation facilitate the method of appropriating one's history? It brings the element of mystery (Christ's life and my own) into prominence.
4. How does the activity of appropriating one's history help one to contemplate? It encourages one to reflect on the significance of the historical in Jesus' life in reference to one's own life.

One major advantage to viewing my history as matter for contemplation is found in the stance that I take to my own story. In contemplating, I approach my life as a mystery; I view myself in the light of the continual presence and activity of God. There arises an increased awareness of the mystery of my own life and this awareness becomes an element in the consolation of my history.

The new-found awareness within myself of the importance of my history suffers when I lose the presence of its mystery. The Church in her concern over specialization in the modern world recognizes the avoidance of mystery and disregard of contemplation (*cf. Vatican II* pg. 206). She insists all the more that there is a great need for a sense of contemplation today (*cf. Vatican II* pg. 261). She encourages me to face life primarily as a mystery to be lived rather than a problem to be solved.

When I am problem oriented, I tend to be alone or at best to form part of a task force tackling the problem. Everything and everyone, even myself, become an object of the end. I see myself as attacking the problem of life in one of two ways.

Either I am the hero who sets out to conquer the problem of life achieving success by strength and power; or I play the anti-hero who accepts life in defeatism with the excuse that life is just a meaningless game. The net result of this problem-solving approach is that it is experienced as impersonal and depressing.

On the other hand, if life is approached as mystery, my negative and positive internal reactions can be judged in terms of personal relationships. Sometimes a negative reaction might be a good and correct one. At other times, it would be evil and incorrect. The same applies to positive reactions. Mystery provides a different perspective for judging reactions than problem solving does.

The sense of mystery allows me to cooperate with others for their sake as well as for my own. Law and order help me, and at times control me so that I can be concerned for others. I reflect on my historical development in a different context. I am interested in the psychological and sociological aspects of my history because they reveal mystery to me, the mystery of myself and of those around me. I experience this revelation as freeing, and as enabling me to be the person my truest desires inspire.

Another advantage in contemplating my history is the very method of prayer that I employ. In place of analysis, introspection, or reasoning, as in the method of meditation, contemplation is the attempt to be present at the mystery of my life and to let God reveal its significance to me. It is the same type of presence and guidance I need in being present to Christ in the mysteries of his life. I cannot claim to know the mystery of my own life anymore than I can claim to know the mystery of his life. There is a parallel revelation going on. God reveals the mystery of my life to me at the same time he is revealing the mystery of Christ's life to me.

Two ways of contemplating can be employed when I wish to appropriate my history in faith. One way is to contemplate the mysteries of Christ's earthly life as passed on by the believing community through scripture. In this method I concentrate on the mystery of Christ's life as present to me during reflection and draw fruit for myself. Indirectly, this means that I may be contemplating my own life while praying within the mystery of Christ's earthly life. There is a parallel revelation going on. Christ reveals myself to me at the same time that he is revealing himself to me.

The second way of contemplating is to focus specifically on the love of God in my own life. In this method I am more directly considering the elements of my life as an expression of God's unique love for me. It is a more immediate contemplation of the mystery of my unique life events. It suits the growing awareness of my own history. Traditionally, such contemplation is most beneficial after many hours of contemplating the mysteries of the earthly life of Christ. Today, this second way might better precede the contemplations of Christ's life, at least in some form or other because people need the assurance that God loves them personally.

What follows is an experience from my own life. It contains certain elements of both ways of contemplating. I'll treat the first way, then later, the second, and more direct, way of contemplating my life. This latter is a study of St. Ignatius' "Contemplation to Attain the Love of God" as an exercise to aid me in appropriating my history, and, with the accompanying consolation, to come to correct decisions with the Lord.

Contemplating My Own Life's History

This section of the chapter will be a brief example of how I have contemplated my own life since 1972. The impact of that year has changed my prayer approach from that of meditation to contemplation. The example will serve as an introduction to this method of appropriating one's history in faith.

Meditating over my life had given me the insight that my whole life is valuable, that my own history is salvific. It is to be loved and understood as a continual experience with God. I realize that God is the giver rather than the demander. This frees me to contemplate the grace of my history. It is similar to the way in which meditations on sin give me the insight that I am loved as I am, and, in turn, free me to contemplate the mysteries of Christ's life in order to love and follow him more closely.

With the 1972 experience there occurred a shift from mere

admiration for the founder of my religious order to one of fellowship with him. My sense of well-being at that time came from the encouragement of an experienced intimacy with Jesus and gave me the realization that all had not been wasted. My life's history was valuable, meaningful, and significant for the future. I began evaluating my life-history differently. I now perceived that my whole life contained the element of mystery.

Mystery is not limited to moments of religious experience. Before 1972, I had often reflected on various experiences of spiritual delight and meaningfulness, of sorrow and tears over my lack of fidelity to the religious life, of joy at seeing others relate to Christ. I think in particular of the many experiences of tears I had at the Eucharist in the late 1960's when praying, "Lamb of God, you take away the sins of the world, have mercy on me". Such individual experiences were appreciated. But I had not put them together as parts of one mystery, the unique mystery of my own life.

Gradually, I was led to realize that my life can be considered to parallel these significant events of Jesus' life that we term "Christ's mysteries", and also his whole life's history which is the paschal mystery. I know now that the contemplation of Christ's life helped me to see the unity in the mystery of my own life. The traditional Ignatian method of contemplating the mysteries of Christ urged me to see Christ's life in its wholeness as an historical unity:

. . . to see and consider what they (Jesus, Mary and Joseph) are doing, for example, making the journey and laboring that our Lord might be born in extreme poverty, and that after many labors, after hunger, thirst, heat, and cold, after insults and outrages, He might die on the cross, and all this for me. Then I will reflect (on myself) and draw some spiritual fruit from what I have seen.

. . . The sixth will be to call to mind frequently the mysteries of the life of Christ our Lord from the Incarnation to the place or mystery I am contemplating [*116, 130*].

In the process of contemplating my own life I began first with those events I was able to recall in which the action of grace (being blest) appeared more obvious, and then moved on to an appreciation of my whole life as blest. "What do you have that was not given to you?" (1 Co. 4:7). The experiences were my own. Yet, more and more, I realized their significance for other persons in my life. So by using the simple contemplative method of seeing who the persons were and what they were saying and doing, an awareness of their blest influence on my whole life grew. I contemplated even more deeply as I saw the historical connection between the events of my life and those of Jesus and his Paschal Mystery.

Besides the four incidents recounted in Chapter 2, I can recall my sense of mystery, awe and worship at mass, and how privileged I felt as an adolescent, in comparison with the rest of my family and my non-Catholic friends. At other times, mystery was experienced in the fragile sense of existence, in tears of sorrowful gratitude as I experienced my own continual existence after sinning. I realized the activity of the Holy Spirit in incidents of my life where I was drawn beyond my normal reactions—transcending them. Where formerly I might have felt threatened by the demands or non-belief of others or envious at their talents, I could now relate kindly, compassionately, openly, humbly, admiringly. Thanks to an insight from a spiritual counsellor, I was able to appreciate the advice and results of Jesus' words: ". . . do not worry beforehand about what to say; no, say whatever is given to you when the time comes, because it is not you who will be speaking: it will be the Holy Spirit" (Mk. 13:11).

Other experiences of God's presence in those whom I was counselling and with whom I was sharing the good news of Jesus brought me a sense of spiritual joy. I was surprised that I could be God's instrument in this way. I could rejoice with the seventy-two disciples reporting to Jesus and I could appreciate his prayer: "I bless you, Father, Lord of heaven and earth, for hiding these things from the learned and the clever and revealing them to mere children" (Lk. 10:21). I saw these experiences as gifts from God, and so I reflected upon myself in these incidents of my life and compared them to the mysteries of Christ's life.

As I contemplate these events I am aware of the presence of blest persons in my life. The Trinity's unique relationship with me comes to me through the love and faith of many persons. In contemplating, I see them again, hear them, observe their goodness, love, sorrow, sufferings and joys as they influence me. There is the mystery of my father's years of suffering. At once well-liked, yet dogged by a sense of inferiority, he turned to alcohol. He was unfailingly kind to my widowed aunt in the midst of all his own sorrow. It was hard to miss his gentleness, his admiration of others and his hospitality to priests. There is the mystery of my mother's patience with her drinking husband, her continual love for him, her strength and laughter. There is the mystery of my friendship with the Dominican Sisters in my adolescence, my admiration of Oblate, Basilian, Redemptorist and Jesuit priests before entering the Society of Jesus, and my further discussions with friends and advisors in my own order.

In my more recent years a new element of affectivity and spiritual joy has come through the persons—priests, sisters, laity—I have guided in retreats. There is present to me the mystery of the inter-dynamic of one or two persons of faith in my life, as well as the mystery of faith communities. I recall the years of dialogue with the Jesuit novice-masters of North America in the 1960's, and the development of the personally-directed Spiritual Exercises apostolate. I recall how this impetus was picked up and supported by the community at Loyola House and Ignatius College, Guelph. I see the presence of the Holy Spirit particularly in the very human elements of these persons and communities and the direction of my history contained in my living with them.

I feel drawn to contemplate my life even more when I experience God explicitly using me to benefit others. For example, I have sometimes become aware of some weakness or instruction given to me in my own life, a day or two before it became applicable to another person. I recall the incident of discussing with a friendly counsellor my painful need for approval as a preacher and, through dialogue, discovering this need was related to the humiliating experiences during my

Jesuit formation while I was trying to read or preach before the Jesuit community. Three days later, I was counselling someone else with a similar dread of standing up before an audience with stage fright and presenting matter she knew very well. Discussing my own humiliating experience and nervousness in terms of Christ's and Paul's similar experience became a help for this other person.

In more recent years I have begun to see these incidents as part of the continuous whole of God's unique love for me throughout my life. Thus, I have become more and more taken up with contemplating the mystery of Jesus' humanity and his relationship with his parents, friends, teachers, scribes, pharisees, romans and apostles. The value of his human life and its direction became a paradigm for my own. Through the mysteries of the life of this human being, Jesus, and of other persons used by the Holy Spirit during Jesus' life and my own, I was able truly "to reflect upon myself and draw some fruit from what has been seen, heard".

Contemplating the mystery of these relationships I see how different persons and communities of faith brought me from a degree-centered, financially solvent, country club attitude towards life, to a surrender to the "unrealistic" demands of a vocation to the Jesuits. I also see how the Spirit spoke to me through my Jesuit friends when I failed the comprehensive examination in philosophy. I am aware now of how the faith and example of my tertian-master supported me in my determination to be compassionate, trusting, and open with the novices. This persisted even though in the concrete situation I saw that mature cooperation, dedication, generosity, and understanding were not always present among the novices themselves.

Contemplating the presence of such people in my life has led to another awareness—the way in which the Lord has allowed me to be more and more in touch with the inner mystery of other persons trying to discover their vocation or apostolic direction. My own experience of inadequacy, aloneness, alienation and fear, along with great desire and longing for Christ, became a means of sympathy, compassion and insight in directing others in retreats. Thus, I have experienced much surprise at the success of the apostolate at Loyola House, Guelph, between 1969 and 1977, and at the approval of workshops there and elsewhere—all the while constantly being aware that it is not my doing. The results are so far beyond my own ability, yet present in spite of my sins and sinfulness. The significance of Paul's words come home: "Not by anything of your own, but by a gift from God; not by anything that you have done, so that nobody can claim the credit. We are God's work of art" (Eph. 2:9:10).

There is obviously more to relate about the contemplation of my life as a mystery of blessings. I hope that these examples will indicate something of the method I used. It is that of reflecting upon the personal relationships in my own life, in conjunction with the mysteries of Christ's life, and seeing the parallel blessings and paradoxes as suggested in the contemplations on the public life of Christ.

When contemplating the mystery of one's whole life, then, these aspects are important: the experiences of paradox, mystery, the transcendent; the experience of going beyond self (transcending myself); where Jesus has been present; how the Holy Spirit has been coming to me and leading me through other persons; how I see my life as intimately part of the Trinity's life.

Ignatius' Final Contemplation

The second way of contemplating has a more direct approach to the mystery of my history, as well as to other features that are important in appropriating my history in faith. Since such contemplation leads me to seek and find God in all things, it affords an experience of true spiritual consolation. This second way of contemplating my history is presented in St. Ignatius' final "Contemplation to Attain the Love of God."

This contemplation has been very significant in my own life. It complements what I have said about my life. It has helped me to contemplate and appropriate my history. But it has many ramifications and so I will treat them at length.

Besides offering another context of appropriation, the

study of this contemplation can achieve three things: it can expose yet more clearly what is meant by the appropriation of one's history in faith; it can introduce this specialized method of appropriation to the reader; it can help the reader to make and appreciate this kind of contemplation as a living and ongoing way of praying.

The Ignatian exercise serves as such a good example of a contemplative appropriation exercise that it will be presented here in its entirety.

CONTEMPLATION TO ATTAIN THE LOVE OF GOD

Note: Before presenting this exercise it will be good to call attention to two points:

1. The first is that love ought to manifest itself in deeds rather than in words.

2. The second is that love consists in a mutual sharing of goods, for example, the lover gives and shares with the beloved what he possesses, or something of that which he has or is able to give; and vice versa, the beloved shares with the lover. Hence, if one has knowledge, he shares it with the one who does not possess it; and also if one has honors, or riches. Thus, one always gives to the other.

**Prayer:* The usual prayer.

First Prelude: This is the representation of the place, which here is to behold myself standing in the presence of God our Lord and of His angels and saints, who intercede for me.

Second Prelude: This is to ask for what I desire. Here it will be to ask for an intimate knowledge of the many blessings received, that filled with gratitude for all, I may in all things love and serve the Divine Majesty.

***First Point:* This is to recall to mind the blessings of creation and redemption, and the special favors I have received.

I will ponder with great affection how much God our Lord has done for me, and how much He has given me of what He possesses, and finally, how much as far as He can, the same Lord desires to give Himself to me according to His divine decrees.

Then I will reflect upon myself, and consider, according to all reason and justice, what I ought to offer the Divine Majesty, that is, all I possess and myself with it. Thus, as one would do who is moved by great feeling, I will make this offering of myself.

Take, Lord, and Receive

Take, Lord, and receive all my liberty, my memory, my understanding, and my entire will, all that I have and possess. Thou hast given all to me. To Thee, O Lord, I return it. All is Thine, dispose of it wholly according to Thy will. Give me Thy love and Thy grace, for this is sufficient for me.

Second Point: This is to reflect how God dwells in creatures: in the elements giving them existence, in the plants giving them life, in the animals conferring upon them sensation, in man bestowing understanding. So He dwells in me and gives me being, life, sensation, intelligence; and makes a temple of me, since I am created in the likeness and image of the Divine Majesty.

Then I will reflect upon myself again in the manner stated in the first point, or in some other way that may seem better.

The same should be observed with regard to each of the points given below.

Third Point: This is to consider how God works and labors for me in all creatures upon the face of the earth, that is, He conducts Himself as one who labors. Thus, in the heavens, the elements, the plants, the fruits, the cattle, etc., He gives being, conserves them, confers life and sensation, etc.

Then I will reflect on myself.

Fourth Point: This is to consider all blessings and gifts as descending from above. Thus, my limited power comes from the supreme and infinite power above, and so, too, justice, goodness, mercy, etc., descend from above as the rays of light descend from the sun, and as the waters flow from their fountains, etc.

Then I will reflect on myself, as has been said.

Conclude with a colloquy and the *Our Father.* [230-237]

* "I will beg God our Lord for the grace that all my intentions, actions, and operations may be directed purely to the praise and service of His Divine Majesty" [46].

**The First, Second, Third, and Fourth Point of this contemplation will be referred to in this book as the first, second, third and fourth movement.

The initial stance in this contemplation is to "behold myself standing in the presence of God our Lord and of His angels and saints, who intercede for me" [232]. This gives the setting in which a person can find God in all things. It is an atmosphere of consolation—surrounded by the saints who have triumphed. Courage, faith, and hope begin the quest. It may help to recall the words of the author of the Hebrews: "With so many witnesses in a great cloud on every side of us, we too, then should throw off everything that hinders us, especially the sin that clings so easily, and keep running steadily in the race we have started. Let us not lose sight of Jesus, who leads us in our faith and brings it to perfection." (Heb. 12:1,2).

As "I ask for what I desire", there takes place a movement from heaven to myself. I am also one of the blessed, even now. I should "Ask for an intimate knowledge of the many blessings received, that filled with gratitude for all, I may in all things love and serve the Divine Majesty" [233]. This opening petition indicates that it is in the context of grateful knowledge about God's love for me from the past events in my life that I will serve God more discreetly in the future.

The consolation that I am seeking in this contemplation will come from a knowledge of my blest history. This consideration of my past also establishes a hope for the future. The "intimate knowledge of the many blessings received," implies the awareness of my unique history in God's plan of things. It encompasses the history of who I am up to now: a member of the human race, of this culture with my Christian faith, in this family and community, and with this vocation. It includes the sense of tradition that has been given to me by my family, my nation, my culture, my church and its relationship to both the Old and New Testament, or by all the traditions of my spouse's family, or by those of the religious community I've joined. The statement, "That I may in all things love and serve", suggests that I can find in my history the kind of love God has for me and that this love will serve me in the future. It is a love that is alive and growing, yet permanent. It is a covenant love.

What is the consolation called "intimate knowledge of the many blessings received", and how is it experienced? It is similar to the wisdom Paul speaks about, a wisdom that is the glorious favor of God and opens up to us the mystery and plan of my own life. Paul says, "He has let us know the mystery of his purpose, the hidden plan he so kindly made in Christ" (Eph. 1:9). He prays, "May the God of our Lord Jesus Christ, the Father of glory, give you a spirit of wisdom and perception of what is revealed . . . . May he enlighten the eyes of your mind so that you can see what hope his call holds for you" (Eph. 1:17, 18). If this contemplation is to involve the mystery of my person and God's plan, then it will have to go beyond an impersonal assent to the truths contained in the plan, and even beyond the acknowledgement of the individual acts of God's care for me, as important as these are. It will include my whole life's history which I carry with me.

The consolation of an intimate knowledge of the many blessings received which is given to me while contemplating my life, is experienced differently at different times. One type of experience may be strictly spatial. The expression, "all things", refers to what I feel, see, and touch. Other experiences may be more historical and have to do with my relationships. At another time, I might experience it as a general wrap-up of all the truths gained throughout a prolonged prayer experience such as a deep assent to the truth that God has loved me in the past evoking gratitude in the present and the desire to love him more in the future. This may give a great sense of certitude to my belief in God. A later experience of this contemplation might uncover a new significance in the words "intimate knowledge"; they may come to mean "deep-felt" or "heart-felt" knowledge, or knowledge that is passionate and born of love. The biblical use of the word "to know", as scripture scholars point out, carries with it these affective dimensions. The biblical statement, "Adam knew his wife" (*cf.* Gn. 4:1) is an example of this usage in a most physical sense.

When the contemplation of my life "comes alive", I am able to recall with deep affection the series of events in my life where I have experienced the special blessings of God. I know at the moment of contemplating that God is the one who showers me with blessings. Still, the understanding of the style of God's relationship with me may not be present. My spiritual life may be experienced as a cycle of sin, forgiveness, gratitude, love, service; then sin, forgiveness, gratitude, love, service, again and again. I may find it difficult to see any growth. I might give up any attempt at understanding my special pattern of life-relationship with God.

But when I experience the consolation of spiritual understanding, and I realize that God has a unique personal and historical relationship with me, my contemplation has already changed or is changing. Then it takes on an interpersonal element it didn't have when it was a matter of contemplating the beauty of creation and persons, or of reflecting on eternal truths, or of being a recall of a number of individual blessings. It is experienced as new because I am contemplating the pattern of my whole life in the living plan of God.

Sometimes the consolation of "intimate knowledge" of God's love for me is experienced in flights of mystical prayer while I am contemplating my life. At other times, it is encountered in the quiet awareness that God is present in all the things I see, hear, smell, taste, and touch. Another instance of this experience is the knowledge that my whole life's history is gathered up in God's love. This means that my history is appreciated in the experience of God's love. Such appreciation can also be verified on different levels. It is alive and growing as are all love relationships.

I often consider my sense of God as an independent set of

actions that I perform for him. But what does my contemplating of Jesus as the paradigm of my life tell me? The Father was constantly present with Jesus and approving his personal decisions and actions. Contemplating my own life in relationship with God gives me the realization that my service of God is not an impersonal, cold duty. My very life in all its historical manifestations is an intimate expression of my service of God.

Such an experience of the consolation of my history seems to fulfill my need for "intimate knowledge". It is a knowledge of the heart which is gained by God's special grace moving me. For it is God's grace that enables me to remember the blessings of his love for me in the past, and fill these remembrances with the intimacy that is his self-communication to me. This intimacy compounds an experience of being loved with that of remembering the previous love acts of God for me. It suggests the knowledge of a love that is constantly present and constantly given because God is always faithful and true to the totality of his existence (a covenant love). But it also indicates a unique love for me, love which is contained in the many "historical" blessings I have received. Such knowledge is more than the experiences of particular consolations. It is a knowledge of the relationship of my whole life with God: a knowledge that is cumulative and manifests what I call the pattern of God's intimate love-relationship with me.

Contemplating and reflecting on my life shows up characteristics of God's relationship with me. Contemplating a mystery of Christ's life gives different insights to different persons which fit the pattern of relationship each one has with God. The pattern may include God's way of answering a person's need for patience or activity, for gentleness or strength, etc.; it also expresses the historical way God draws and urges a person to intimacy with him in all things.

This intimacy that I appreciate as the expression of my whole life naturally leads to the second part of the petition: "that filled with gratitude for all, I may in all things love and serve the Divine Majesty". The consolation of knowing God's many blessings is the force that takes my gratitude and moves it into decisions and actions. For decisions and actions are the stuff of love. The words, "in all things", include the historical. The love of God is in all things of my past as well as in my future. The understanding of the pattern of God's intimate love-relationship that I see in my history as a social being of this family, of the human race, of western culture, of this nation, church, parish, religious community, is living and growing. It is always moving me into the future as indicated in the words, "love and serve the Divine Majesty". The movement proceeds from intimate knowledge through gratitude to love and service.

My love and service of the Divine Majesty in all things is helped by this intimate knowledge of my history and its accompanying consolation for two reasons. The first is based on my freedom to love, and the consequent possibility of turning away from that love, that is, of sinning. My freedom, of course, has been given so I can cooperate responsibly with God's activity in my daily life. The consolation of my history gives me that modern sense of myself as historical. This consolation, together with my past experiences, is the reality on which I am to make free decisions for the future. The second reason is to prevent my being deceived by the immediate experience of a particular good. Because this consolation of my history appropriates my past, it includes an intimate knowledge of how I sinned and was deceived in the past. Such an appropriation is important for the recognizing, understanding, and avoiding of deceptions in the future.

One method of discerning how best to love and serve God is based on my sensing whether a decision is in keeping with true spiritual consolation. The intimate knowledge of God's comprehensive and persisting love throughout my history can be the exemplar (paradigm) of true spiritual consolation. When my desire to serve Christ is present, I can ask myself whether the decision leaves me in a peace that harmonizes with the consolation of my own history and the trend that I perceive in it.

The offering prayer, "Take, Lord, and Receive" all I possess and myself with it, expresses an openness to love and serve in the future. Such an offering is closely related to the consolation gained from a consideration of historical blessings I have received. The emphasis that is placed on the self-communication of God and of "how much, as far as He can, the same Lord desires to give Himself to me" refers to interpersonal historical knowledge. When I offer myself in turn, I offer my memory, and thus my historical remembrances. I am then engaged in the activity of appropriating my history in faith for it has become a part of me; and, aware of God's continual presence with me in the past, I offer it in trust and confidence for the future.

The element of spiritual consolation necessary for loving and serving God is present when I ponder my history, because the consolation of my history accompanies the appropriation. This is so when the desire for "an intimate knowledge of the many blessings received" contains the historical experience of repentance and transforming union with Christ. Contemplating my life includes the experience of previous prayer exercises and the sentiment of amazing gratitude that I am a forgiven sinner; it provides the intimate knowledge of Christ needed for love and service in building the kingdom; and it adds to these my future desire to love and serve the Lord in all things. The appropriation of these recent prayer experiences as part of my history is attained in this contemplation of the mystery of my life.

Ignatius' Final Contemplation and the Phases of Appropriation

The two ways of contemplating one's history have been presented. Now I will discuss more specifically the interrelationship of the "Contemplation to Attain the Love of God" and the activity of appropriating one's history in faith. It has been noted that this contemplation can be considered as a beginning exercise in appropriating one's history or as a developing exercise. In both instances it enlightens the person praying for appropriation. When this contemplation is a beginning exercise in appropriation, it is quite straight forward and progresses according to the four movements. When it is a developing exercise in a series of exercises bringing about appropriation, the interplay of the four phases of the activity of appropriation with the four movements of this contemplation is more complex. Moreover, the format is helpful in organizing and explaining the activity of appropriating one's history in faith. The contemplation contains the activity of appropriating one's history and conversely the activity of appropriating enhances this contemplation. This can be seen by comparing the four movements of this contemplation with the four phases of appropriating: remembering, searching, being whole, being open.

When this contemplation becomes a prayer exercise that introduces the appropriating of my history, it is usually the influence of the first movement that encourages this. Here I am instructed to "recall to mind the blessings of creation and redemption, and the special favors I have received." This remembering of my history is done in an intimate context of the mystery of God's abiding love as I am asked to "ponder with great affection how much God our Lord has done for me, and . . . how much, as far as He can, the same Lord desires to give Himself to me."

In the previous prayer exercises I have already been invited to pray over my creaturehood, sinfulness, and call. I am already aware of these aspects of my history. My contemplating now brings everything together and fosters great intimacy with the God of creation, God of mercy, the God who calls. The blessings of creation, redemption and special favors are gathered together under the aspect of God's self-communication to me in the past and all the promises for the future that are contained in that history. This moves me from recalling blessings to a sense of the value of my history, and from there to a trustful and hopeful surrender of everything to God who loves me and my history. My history has value for me not only because I have been shown how it is blessed and loved by God but because I see my history united to God's acts of creation and redemption.

With such a beginning the rest of this contemplation becomes a furthering of the activity of appropriating my history. The words of the second movement, "So He dwells in me . . . and makes a temple of me", lead me to search out the ways (pattern) in which God is present to me. And the awareness that God "labors for me . . . that is, He conducts Himself as one who labors" in the third movement brings forth the consideration of

God's responsibility to me, so that I'm moved to a sense of wholeness and responsibility for my life. Also my awareness from the fourth movement that, "my limited power . . . justice, goodness, mercy, etc., descend from above as rays of light from the sun," opens me up in hope for the future.

To say with meaning the offering prayer, "Take, Lord, and Receive", can lead to an appropriation of my history. The words, "my liberty, my memory, my understanding, and my entire will", do not refer to abstract concepts but to aspects of myself that are realized historically. To say this prayer without some reflection upon my history could be a mere recitation of words. The offering is not meant to be made on the basis of blind belief. Remembering and searching are implied in the words, "Thou hast given all to me". The phase of being whole is present in the words, "To Thee, O Lord, I return it," for there is an acceptance of one's whole life as from God. Being open to the future is quite evident in the last two sentences: "All is Thine, dispose of it wholly according to Thy will. Give me Thy love and Thy grace, for this is sufficient for me".

So it is that this contemplation can become an introduction to the activity of appropriating my history. The four movements can now be seen as a possible format for this activity. Each movement highlights a phase of the activity of appropriating. From this point of view, the phase of remembering one's history is most dominant in the first movement of this contemplation, the phase of searching in the second movement, the phase of being whole in the third movement, the phase of being open in the fourth.

Further understanding is gained when I look at the influence the appropriating of my history and its accompanying consolation has on this contemplation. How do the four phases of appropriation enhance the contemplation when it is the final exercise in a prolonged series of prayer exercises that develop my appropriation? The recalling of blessings now takes on an historical dimension. God's desire to give himself is appreciated in an historical perspective, as I search out his advances of love. The presence of God in all things includes a historical presence as he enters into my history and acts in it to help me perform virtuous acts. In this historical perspective I now experience a wholeness concerning my life because I see that God who has revealed his faithfulness to me up to the present will continue to be faithful in my future and so I make the offering in a feeling of trust and openness.

From the experience of God's intimate and unique love for me expressed in my history I can move to another level of appropriation. This level is not just an act of gratitude for blessings received. It is an act of loving what God has achieved. This loving act includes all my being, past, present, and future. At this level I acknowledge with love that God's unique and intimate dialogue with me in the past has made me what I am. This, I accept with love and then open myself to the future, because I know that he will be with me where my history takes me.

The historical dimension makes each movement of this contemplation a new experience. Thus, I realize in the first movement that creation, redemption and special favors are ongoing blessings of that covenant love-life with the Lord who has given and wishes to give so much to me, especially himself. The consolation sought and experienced is related to the continual presence of God throughout my own history. I no longer have to work to achieve acceptance or value. I see in this intimate recall that I belong, that I am valuable, that I am blessed. I perceive in this reflection the continuing nature of God's relationship to me, and all the blessings he has given to me. This confirms my belief that he wishes to give me much more of the same.

The first phase of remembering in the appropriating now influences all of this contemplation. As the consideration of personal call, and the desire to know and love and follow Christ in the contemplations of Jesus' public life naturally flows from the remembered experience of sin and God's forgiveness, so a new state of being and an openness to the future flows from this personal remembrance. The movement in the next three parts of this contemplation builds on this remembrance of the first part.

In the second phase when I am searching out the pattern of my life with God, the remembrance of past blessings in the first movement gives me a further appreciation of the second as I ponder how "He dwells in me and gives me life". I see how he strengthens certain virtues over others, how he reveals my sinfulness from one angle rather than another, how he gives particular blessings to me. I discover a recurring emphasis and trend in God's relationship to me. The searching continues on into the labors of God and the virtues given to me as I consider the third and fourth movements. More and more I appreciate the pattern I am discovering.

The third phase of being whole involves taking responsibility for my whole life in a positive way. Such an attitude also helps me to link up all my remembered blessings from the first movement into the historical whole. And my awareness of God continually dwelling in me from the second movement, as well as the appreciation of freedom and responsibility coming through a consideration of the third and fourth, become part of the experience of wholeness.

The fourth phase involves an openness to the forward direction of my history. The words from the first movement: "how much, as far as He can, the same Lord desires to give Himself to me according to His divine decrees", ring true to me. From my past I see that God is constant in his faithfulness and I know that this will continue. When I reflect on the constant pattern of God's indwelling from the second movement, on the constant manner with which God has labored for me in the third and on the experiences of how God's gifts come down to me from the fourth movement I am further opened to the direction which I perceive in my history.

When this contemplation is approached as the final exercise in a retreat that includes the appropriation of my history in faith, then the previous prayer exercises on sin are experienced in a new perspective. In the previous consideration of my sins, my prayer led me to amazement and gratitude that I still exist and am forgiven. My life history suggested that this should not be. I saw the saving act of Jesus very clearly and I prayed for a deep knowledge of my sin, of disorder, and of the world, that I might amend my life. The presence of Jesus on the cross dominated my life history as I appropriated it at this time of prayer.

Now, in this contemplation my sinful history has been brought together with my blessed history, and has been put into the context of God's activity of creation and redemption, which affectively relates my life to Jesus' own life and to his Paschal Mystery.

Similarly as I reflect on the presence of God in all things during the second movement of this contemplation my previous prayer on Jesus' public life is experienced anew. These earlier prayer exercises were dominated by the contemplation on Christ's Incarnation—the great mystery of God becoming man and dwelling among us so that I, like Jesus, might serve the Trinity. The horrifying experience of my sinful history along with God's continual forgiveness gave me a first understanding of my history. The contemplations on the mysteries of Christ's public life and the significance of Jesus' humanity, his identity with me as a human being, provided a further understanding of my history. Now in this contemplation, after considering Jesus' passion and resurrection, I am encouraged to search out the pattern of my history in terms of Jesus' total history, the paschal mystery. As the Spirit was in Jesus throughout his history so I believe that God "dwells in me and gives me life . . . and makes a temple of me". In this contemplation I am led to accept that this includes all my history.

When God is remembered as laboring in his creation in the third movement of this contemplation the previous prayer exercises over the great labor of Christ who suffered and died for me are also recalled. All of the labors I have so recently experienced in prayer as a creature, a sinner going through desolation and darkness to consolation and light, can be related to God's work in me. My own suffering history down the years can even be appropriated as part of God's labor for me.

Awareness of God's gifts descending and coming within me is sought in the fourth movement. If this occurs, the experience of recent contemplations on the resurrection appearances of Jesus will be present, and this will aid me in remembering how he goes about consoling his friends. The phase of being open to the forward direction of my history can now become operative. The ability to console and to go beyond myself is a grace from the contemplations on the risen life of Jesus. The power of the Risen Lord who gives meaning to all the historical events of my creaturely, sinful, suffering life helps me to be open to the virtues I see operating in my history. Humility accompanies this openness to the future as I recall John the Baptist's words: "A man can lay claim only to what is given him from heaven" (Jn. 3:27).

THE ROLE OF THE SPIRITUAL DIRECTOR

The following brief comments are intended to help a spiritual director come to more fully developed principles in guiding others to contemplate their own history.

A. Encourage the awareness of mystery

The director should encourage those being directed to recognize and locate those moments of mystery in their life. What is first experienced as a problem event may be considered from the viewpoint of mystery. The director should encourage the one being directed to taste and relish, to wonder and appreciate rather than to analyze and solve. Encouraged in this way, the person being directed will often become aware of constantly receiving from God the help that was needed to understand and to make adjustments in life so as to live more fully or choose more wisely. This awareness of mystery will more easily be encouraged with events that are experienced as peak or transcendent experiences. Paradoxical experiences may also be the basis for this growing awareness of mystery.

B. Encourage different aspects of appropriation

As the person shifts from meditation to contemplation, the director will be attentive to perceive and encourage different aspects of appropriation. Such encouragement always should follow the lead of the Spirit.

The director will encourage the one being directed to return to those aspects of a previous contemplation where there may have emerged continuity of life, a sense of development, or appreciation of the historical in Jesus' life. For example, suppose the person were contemplating the call of the apostles from John's gospel and the words of Nathaniel, "From Nazareth? Can anything good come from that place?" stirred up a long line of personal historical events. The director could perhaps encourage the person to return to this part of prayer and to bring these events back into the presence of the gospel mystery as a means of comparison.

When the person being directed has received the sense that all of one's life is a mystery, the director should explain the dynamic of one or other of the four phases, for example, searching for the pattern which God has been using in these events.

EXERCISE

Praying with the mystery elements in my life

Introduction

Then Jesus appeared: he came from Galilee to the Jordan to be baptized by John. John tried to dissuade him. "It is I who need baptism from you," he said, "and yet you come to me!" But Jesus replied, "Leave it like this for the time being; it is fitting that we should, in this way, do all that righteousness demands." At this, John gave in to him.

As soon as Jesus was baptized he came up from the water, and suddenly the heavens opened and he saw the Spirit of God descending like a dove and coming down on him. And a voice spoke from heaven, "This is my Son, the Beloved, my favor rests on him." (Mt. 3:13-17)

This was a very significant spirit experience for Jesus. In the light of this experience he could recapitulate the thirty years of living in Nazareth. It prepared him for much of his life that was to follow.

I too have important experiences in my life that can help me contemplate the continual presence of God between these significant moments.

Suggested Approaches

I seek the grace to be present to my life history as it is loved by God, and I pray that I may respond more generously to the love of God flooding my heart.

I begin by asking God to help me to locate one sensed moment of mystery in my life.

I might look at moments in my life that are quiet but filled with affection for God . . . those times of hope for myself and my life as loved by God . . . the times when I see my life as valuable to others . . . the times when I have experienced generosity, compassion, peace, welling-up in me.

I might be drawn immediately to a moment of peak religious experience of God, a moment of conversion, insight, joy, sorrow, flowing from the felt-presence of God.

From these, I pray to be able to contemplate the continual presence of God between these significant spiritual events that I now recognize as mystery so that God will give me the spiritual felt-insight of how he has been continually present to me and is leading me.

5 THE PHASE OF REMEMBERING

Remember your kindness, Yahweh,
your love, that you showed long ago.
Do not remember the sins of my youth;
but rather, with your love remember me.

Yahweh is so good, so upright,
he teaches the way to sinners;
in all that is right he guides the humble,
and instructs the poor in his way.

All Yahweh's paths are love and truth
for those who keep his covenant and his decrees.
For the sake of your name, Yahweh,
forgive my guilt, for it is great.

Everyone who fears Yahweh
will be taught the course a man should choose;
his soul will live in prosperity,
his children have the land for their own.
The close secret of Yahweh belongs to them who fear him,
his covenant also, to bring them knowledge. (Ps. 25:6-14)

The previous chapters have introduced the four phases of the activity of appropriating one's unique history in faith. Now the first phase, remembering, will be treated more extensively. Remembering as a phase of appropriation is not complete in itself but interrelates with the other three phases of searching, being whole and being open. A return to this remembering my history occurs as I search for the pattern in my history or as I experience being whole or being open.

This phase is designed to help me appropriate my whole history as I am recalling it and contains its own consolation as distinct from the comprehensive consolation of my total history. It has an attribute that ordinary remembering does not have, the desire to be in touch with my whole history and to accept it as I remember incidents from it.

This remembering is intended also to help me appropriate my life in faith. Thus, my remembering is done in the context of the mystery of my whole life as known and loved by God. It is remembering to find the meaning, significance, and value of my life. It is remembering in the presence of God's abiding love throughout my life. The events of my life are recalled as blessings and as signs of hope for the future.

This is different from the process of recalling certain incidents of my life in order to re-experience traumatic or sinful situations that might be helpful in psychology or in the healing of memories. Such recalling can give me the psychological insight to free myself from a past trauma or face a sinful experience in my past. Sometimes the healing of memories allows persons to hand over to Jesus the heavy load of guilt that is weighing them down. At other times, a new experience of the Lord's personal love frees them to forgive other persons who have rejected or wounded them psychologically. They are given the gift of compassion.

The remembering that we are speaking about, however, would include this recalling and proceed further. For example, after a prayer experience in which there is a healing of memories, persons are often tempted to fear that they will fall back again into the old tendencies of anger or bitterness. This fear may be realized when further experiences of bitterness, anger, or guilt occur. Discouragement, despondency, and lack of faith are the result. Then there is the temptation to deny the original saving activity of God's power to heal or convert, "So that the man ends up by being worse than he was before" (Mt. 12:45).

But this recurring bitterness, anger, or guilt can be the occasion of a new humility and means of spiritual understanding for these people. Now they acknowledge their continual need of the Lord and admit their spiritual poverty and weakness. Often the reason for discouragement and despondency is the desire to be "confirmed in grace", to be healed once and for all, or to be perfect and holy so that one can always be in full control of these tendencies. Now, with humility and insight there may come a willingness to be a developing person in faith and not one in perfect control.

The recurrence of bitterness indicates that the healing of a particular experience of bitterness is not the healing of all such experiences. One healing experience is a gift; when this gift encourages persons to further remember for the sake of spiritual insight they are beginning to appropriate their history.

This further activity of remembering helps them to acknowledge the reality of God's saving and healing powers in the past while allowing for their tendencies to keep recurring. As the memory brings forth more of these personal experiences from the past such persons can see these tendencies in an overall historical setting. Now in meekness, the historical, developmental dimensions of the past can be appreciated, and the recurring of these tendencies, accepted. With the help of God, they can also move away from the tendencies because they see that there are experiences in their past which give hope and that conquest of sinful tendencies is fundamentally a gradual historical process. Thus they grasp some understanding of how the movement to further freedom takes place in their lives.

Although it has the same context of the continuing love of God as does the healing of memories, the phase of remembering in the appropriation of one's history is of a different order. It is an activity for enlightenment and learning. It presumes that life is historical, continuous, and developmental and not a series of isolated incidents. One remembers in order to learn by reflecting on one's life as a total historical experience. Whereas the ministry of healing is more concerned to discover and heal those isolated moments and events which are the source of alienation, anger, hatred, and whatever malformation there is in one's personality, the remembering of one's whole history has for its purpose recognizing interior spiritual movements and using this knowledge in making correct decisions.

Such remembering is not limited to recalling isolated incidents of one's life; it is concerned with remembering incidents in relation to all of life. The context of remembering becomes an important part of the activity. The cultural milieu—family, school, classmates, work, country, wars—influences this remembering. As an example, I am now able to recall my sense of inadequacy attending university in the years when other young people were in the armed forces or in the war effort and at the same time recall the exterior events of those years. Similarly, when I remember in faith, I remember within the total faith community. As an individual member of the Church I remember my own experiences as a person within the scope of the Church's memory. I experience the Church's remembering at the same time as I have my own unique memory of myself. The context of my remembering as a person of faith not only includes the everyday activities of study, work, and recreation but also the faith milieu that declares that I am a child of God and a recipient of salvation history.

So I remember the various events, places, people, responsibilities, delights, successes, and failures of my life, as a person in a community that includes my family, city, nation, world at the particular time. But enfolding all this is the memory of God's actions for humanity in Jesus Christ communicated to me by the Church remembering.

In exercising my memory, I can begin to realize that my reactions to a situation, my understanding of myself, my feelings about myself and others all have an historical aspect. For example, I can say: "That makes sense against the background of the depression of the 1930's or the war of the 1940's or the communications revolution of the 1960's."

In a similar way I understand that the expression of the Church's faith also has an historical aspect, which enters into my individual experience. So when I am remembering the events and persons of my own life, I am also remembering the historical expression of the faith at the time.

Even though my faith's expression is influenced by the

present culture and concerns, its historical aspect is very much present and sometimes in a very special way because of the action of the Holy Spirit in presenting it to me. My faith and its history cannot help but be an integral part of my remembering my personal history.

It is the believing community that is the instrument of the Holy Spirit arousing in me the memory of the good news of Jesus' incarnation, death and resurrection. Paul insists on this: "But they will not ask his help unless they believe in him, and they will not believe in him unless they have heard of him, and they will not hear of him unless they get a preacher, and they will never have a preacher unless one is sent . . . So faith comes from what is preached, and what is preached comes from the word of Christ." (Rm. 10:14-17) I believe by hearing from the believing Church what she remembers. It is within the context of what the Church remembers that my memory is shaped.

Through and in the Church's faith, there is a living memory available to me. As I allow this memory to enter my being, I discover how adaptable this faith is and yet how unique it is for me. Relating the memory of my history to the Church's memory results in a new experience of faith as well as of history.

This faith memory of the believing community influences my remembrance of my own life in that it brings before me the mystery of Jesus' life as an explanation of my life, as a motivation for my life, and as a source of strength for my life. It makes the mystery of Jesus present so that I can respond to the challenge of Paul: "Have that mind in you which was in Christ Jesus" (*cf.* Ph. 2:5). The events of Jesus' life are given in a living way that meets the cultural situation and adapts them for today.

The Church's memory of Jesus resurrected always colors all of my remembering, sometimes more vividly, sometimes less, depending on my awareness at the time. The practice of remembering my own life history while contemplating the mysteries of Jesus' life as remembered by the Church opens my being to further remembering and understanding.

When I situate myself within the Church's memory, I become aware of two aspects in her remembering. The first is a remembering that is dependent on historical data. The second is the kind of remembering that operates in her liturgical celebrations known as *anamnesis*. For appropriating, both aspects of remembering are present, and there will be a movement from one aspect to the other as appropriation proceeds.

The memory of the Church is multifaceted. The Church remembers persons and actions; she remembers saints and great leaders; she remembers persecutions and triumphs. She remembers, in the form of written documents such as her sacred books of the Old and New Testament and through archaeological monuments, the pronouncements of the Councils and the declarations of the Roman Pontiff. This remembering is rightly called history. In the Church's history we have accounts of the great Councils and the state of the Church down through the centuries. The statements of the Church's councils and the declarations of the Roman Pontiff are important for a true presentation of the Church's understanding of herself and so of her memory. The Church's memory of herself is also influenced by the different cultures through which she has existed. The study of the cultural *milieu* and the literary *genre* of her documents is helpful in recalling the historical evidence.

Within the believing community, persons can find help in this remembering from good spiritual directors. Such directors affirm the one being directed when they bring forth the memory of the Church as it is expressed in scripture and the other fonts of tradition. Good directors are careful to judge or present a modern theological understanding of the faith in agreement with the Church's living memory as it is contained in this historical evidence.

But there is another aspect of the Church's memory beyond the recall of historical evidence. It is a memory quite unique to her. It is the memory of the words and actions of Jesus Christ. This special memory is operative at the reading of scripture and in the Eucharistic liturgy. It is a memory that is alive and active. It is even more present than the recall of past events in one's own life. In recent declarations the Church has emphasized the sacramental aspect of the scripture as well as the Eucharist. "Christ is present in His Church especially in her liturgical celebrations. . . . He is present in His word, since it is He Himself who speaks when the Holy Scriptures are read in the Church" (*Vatican II*, pg. 141). When, in faith, I hear or read scripture it is the living word of God for me. This "re-presenting" through remembering of past events is most pronounced in the Eucharist.

Scripture scholars see this same kind of memory operating in Jesus. With the other faithful Israelites, the *anawim*, Jesus celebrates in the present the past deeds of Yahweh, his Father, for the chosen people. "Unrolling the scroll he found the place where it is written: The spirit of the Lord has been given to me, for he has anointed me. He has sent me to bring the good news to the poor, to proclaim liberty to captives and to the blind new sight, to set the downtrodden free, to proclaim the Lord's year of favor. . . . Then he began to speak to them, 'This text is being fulfilled today even as you listen' " (Lk. 4:17-21). The liberation from slavery in Egypt and the words of the prophets are a present reality to Jesus.

A technical term for this kind of remembering in faith is *anamnesis*. In *A Dictionary of Liturgy and Worship*, J. G. Davies says: "*anamnesis* is all but untranslatable into English. Memorial, commemoration, remembrance—all these suggest that the person or deed commemorated is past and absent, whereas *anamnesis* signifies exactly the opposite: it is an objective act, in and by which the person or event commemorated is actually made present, is brought into the realm of the here and now."

One explanation given for this kind of remembering is the presence of the Holy Spirit in each Christian and in the believing community. St. Luke has Our Lady, a type of the Church, "pondering all these things in her heart" (Lk. 2:19). The person pondering scripture has the assistance of the Holy Spirit, "the advocate, the Holy Spirit, whom the Father will send in my name, will teach you everything and remind you of all I have said to you" (Jn. 14:26). The believing community also has the power of the Holy Spirit to accomplish a "re-presentation" of Jesus' life, death, and resurrection at the Eucharistic liturgy, "Do this as a memorial of me" (Lk. 22:19). After the paschal event of the first Easter Sunday, the repetition of the words and gestures of the believing community over bread and wine and the reading aloud of scripture made the saving act of Jesus present again (*cf.* 1 Co. 11:23-29; Jn. 6:53-58).

When as a member of the Church I pray with scripture, I begin by reading the believing community's written account and move back by reflection to the event itself. It is the presence of the Holy Spirit in me that makes the experience live for me. (*cf.* Rom. 8:14-17, 26, 27).

Once I have situated myself within the Church remembering with its two aspects of historical evidence and *anamnesis*, I discover a parallel between the way of contemplating the mysteries of Christ's life and the way of appropriating my history. This parallel comes in the manner that I dispose myself for the grace I am seeking and the experience of the grace received. In contemplating, I recall as the matter of my contemplation the historical as given in the documents of the Church, especially the New Testament Gospels. Then while thinking of the persons in the mystery, what they say and do, I wait for the sense of being present at the mystery which is the experience called *anamnesis*. In appropriating my history I can follow the same process. I dispose myself by recalling the historical data of my life (this includes the data of the Church's history and the data of the history of Christ). With this recall I await the sense of being present at the mystery of my own life, which, again, is an experience of *anamnesis*.

Some of the traditional ways of gathering the historical data of my life are given in the writings of St. Ignatius. In certain instructions for an hour's prayer I am urged to remember elements in my own life. Thus, in prayer over my personal sin, I am instructed to call to mind all the sins of my life, reviewing year by year and period by period and considering the places where I lived, my dealing with others, and the occupations in which I was engaged. Similarly, in a consideration of God's love, I am to recall the blessings of my existence, my salvation, and the special favors received. In the directions for reflection on my prayer I am advised to consider, while sitting or walking for the space of a quarter of an hour, how it went with me during the meditation or contemplation. In the common practice of examining my whole day I am to reflect about myself from the time of rising up to the present time. I am to go over one hour after another, one period after another. When trying to discover more subtle forms of temptation, I am advised to "carefully observe the whole course of our thoughts. If the beginning and middle and end of the course of thoughts are wholly good and directed to what is entirely right, it is a sign that they are from the good angel. But the course of thoughts suggested to us may terminate in something evil . . . These are clear signs that the thoughts are proceeding from the evil spirit" [333].

The example of remembering my sins is a good one because it is done in a faith context, the context in which I have sinned. Faith is the necessary context of sin. So, as I recall my sin, I recall at the same time the Church's faith in God's merciful salvific act accomplished in Jesus' death on the cross for me. I am able to face my sins honestly because of my belief in God's merciful love and my hope in the power of this love which brought life out of death in Jesus' death and resurrection. I know myself as a saved sinner.

Still, I may only recall the historical data as incidents of and not integral to the mystery of my life. Then it is that I seek the sense of remembering from within the mystery of my life—the experience of *anamnesis*.

If I approach my history as an experience of *anamnesis* I seek to know myself as present in the scope of the Church's memory of Christ, "yesterday, today, and the same forever" (*cf.* Heb. 13:8). To do this I go a step beyond the historical recall of incidents in my life. For example, I remember myself historically as a sinner and I pray to put the incidents of my life together. I try to recall further facts about this sin-history as coming from my circle of friends, family, nation, church, from the whole social context of my life. Like Peter's remembering on the lakeshore, I do this remembering from the perspective of the resurrection. The resurrection does not remove Peter's past history. He continues to feel sorrow for denying the Lord, even after the resurrection. But now his sorrow has a new perspective of love (*cf.* Jn. 21:17). So I pray to move in memory from separate incidents to an overall awareness of my whole life. When I do recall events as part of my history, my memory of them becomes new.

For example, the grace to remember my sins as part of my continuing existence and not just as isolated incidents, helps me to be aware of myself as a developing person. When I remember the elements of sin, corruption, and self-destruction, at the same time as my continued existence, I am sensing the mystery of my whole life. I become more and more conscious of a development taking place. My ability to remember in this way is due to the continuing presence of the salvific act of Jesus' death and resurrection—an experience of *anamnesis*.

A further example of the grace of *anamnesis* can occur when the recall of my sins is accompanied by the sense of God's continual presence to me, freeing me from my sins and disorders and calling me beyond them. I remember my life now as a movement away from limitation, disorder, and sin to a response in keeping with my deepest desires. In such remembering I am at joy and peace while at the same time I feel sorrow and tears for my sins.

A third example of the grace of being present to the whole mystery of my life (*anamnesis*) may occur as I recall my sins along with a recall of virtuous acts. The amplified experience of being an instrument of God's love for others, while recalling my sinful acts, leads me into a further appreciation of the mystery of my whole life. I may do an exercise similar to that of the one on personal sin but now recalling the persons, events, responsibilities in which I have been an instrument of God's goodness. This remembering of my grace-filled acts along with my sin-filled acts can be another way of disposing myself for the sense of God's continual presence. The remembering of these opposites as present gives me the awareness of the person developing out of my sins, limitations and spiritual failures towards a loving union with God.

The phase of remembering my history in faith can be achieved if I situate myself within the Church's remembering. I begin by remembering the historical data of my life. While doing this I pray that the Holy Spirit will help me remember my life in terms of Christ's life, death, and resurrection. Appropriation is taking place in such remembering (*anamnesis*) as the sense of being present to my history is experienced.

THE ROLE OF THE SPIRITUAL DIRECTOR

The following comments are intended to help a spiritual director come to more fully developed principles in guiding others through the phase of remembering.

A. Helping the one being directed to remember in the context of faith

The director can help another person be disposed for the sense of consolation through any number of themes—ancestry, creaturehood, growth, social evil, personal evil, call, temptation, desire for good, ambivalence, love for God, union with Jesus, a sense of blessedness. In suggesting these or similar themes the director asks the one being directed to consider them within a faith-context and to pray for enlightenment. This can usually be done with scripture; but the documents of the Church or writings of the saints could also be used. The grace that is being prayed for is to remember one's life with God so as to receive the consolation of the phase, a sense of remembering one's history in faith.

B. Waiting for the consolation of this phase to emerge

The sense of remembering one's history as a consolation may emerge at almost anytime. If the one being directed is in a retreat context, this sense of consolation may come as one is praying through themes of sinfulness or creaturehood; it may emerge at a much later point as one is praying the passion or praying over the blessing of one's own life; or it may only begin to emerge after many retreats. Whether inside or outside the retreat context, the director is always ready to recognize this form of consolation while waiting for the Lord to take the lead.

C. Representing the faith-memory of the believing community

The spiritual director is a representative of the perennial faith-memory of the believing community. The continual appropriation of one's personal history in faith with its concomitant consolation gives the director a sensitivity to this spiritual phenomenon in another. The director listens to the account of the other's history in consonance with the faith-memory of the believing community. He or she has a deep-felt knowledge from within, and is able to confirm the truth of the other person's convictions. The director listens for expressions of this kind: "I am basically good and not rotten because I know that God loves me"; "God is not vindictive in his punishments, but I can be hard-hearted"; "I cannot earn heaven, but I can cooperate freely with God's loving initiatives." There are other expressions that indicate a more historical awareness: "I have grown in patience towards this person and this situation"; "I can see where God has been using my failures, and achieving something quite unexpected, quite beyond my capabilities"; "I know now of God's continuing presence even while I was sinning."

EXERCISE

Remembering with the Lord

Introduction

On the way he came to the Samaritan town called Sychar, near the land that Jacob gave to his son Joseph. Jacob's well is there and Jesus, tired by the journey, sat straight down by the well. It was about the sixth hour. When a Samaritan woman came to draw water, Jesus said to her, "Give me a drink." His disciples had gone into the town to buy food. The Samaritan woman said to him, "What? You are a Jew and you ask me, a

Samaritan, for a drink?" Jews, in fact, do not associate with Samaritans. Jesus replied: "If you only knew what God is offering and who it is that is saying to you: 'Give me a drink,' you would have been the one to ask, and he would have given you living water." "You have no bucket, sir," she answered, "and the well is deep; how could you get this living water? Are you a greater man than our father Jacob who gave us this well and drank from it himself with his sons and his cattle?" Jesus replied: "Whoever drinks this water will get thirsty again; but anyone who drinks the water that I shall give will never be thirsty again; the water that I shall give will turn into a spring inside him, welling up to eternal life." "Sir," said the woman, "give me some of that water, so that I may never get thirsty and never have to come here again to draw water." "Go and call your husband," said Jesus to her, "and come back here." The woman answered, "I have no husband." He said to her, "You are right to say, 'I have no husband'; for although you have had five, the one you have now is not your husband. You spoke the truth there." "I see you are a prophet, sir," said the woman . . .

The woman said to him, "I know that the Messiah—that is, Christ—is coming; and when he comes he will tell us everything." "I who am speaking to you," said Jesus, "I am he." At this point his disciples returned, and were surprised to find him speaking to a woman, though none of them asked, "What do you want from her?" or, "Why are you talking to her?" The woman put down her water jar and hurried back to the town to tell the people, "Come and see a man who has told me everything I ever did; I wonder if he is the Christ?" This brought people out of the town and they started walking toward him . . .

Many Samaritans of that town had believed in him on the strength of the woman's testimony when she said, "He told me all I have ever done," so, when the Samaritans came up to him, they begged him to stay with them. He stayed for two days, and when he spoke to them many more came to believe; and they said to the woman, "Now we no longer believe because of what you told us; we have heard him ourselves and we know that he really is the savior of the world." (Jn. 4:5-19, 25-30, 39-42)

The Samaritan woman was privileged to be with Jesus and he told her everything she ever did. He can do the same thing for me as I open myself to remember.

Suggested Approaches

Beginning with reverence and hope, I look back over my history as the handiwork of the Trinity; I offer to the Trinity the remembering, searching, findings, of this time of prayer.

I ask the Lord to be with me so that I may remember my life's history as an expression of his remembering me. I desire to remember myself as one who has lived continuously in the presence of Jesus knowing me.

Where do I begin? I ask Jesus and I wait. Does he want to tell me, "You are right in saying you have no husband! The fact is you have had five." I don't know where he will begin to remember with me.

Will the remembering begin with my ancestors, with my education, with my family, with special friends? Will it begin with a certain event, a certain person, a certain place, a certain time? Will I recall immediately some deeply emotional experience—one of joy, love, hurt, anger, sorrow? Will I remember those moments of surprise and awe at some religious experience?

My mind moves in an expectation through different experiences of call, promise, fulfilment; of ancestors, natural and spiritual; of journeys, material and spiritual; of sins; of triumphs in the Lord, of testings and pain; of transcending experiences, active and passive.

I am forced to wait and let the Lord lead me in this remembering of my whole life in faith.

6 SEARCHING FOR PATTERN IN ONE'S HISTORY

Take any man who thinks he can rely on what is physical: I am even better qualified. I was born of the race of Israel and of the tribe of Benjamin, a Hebrew born of Hebrew parents, and I was circumcised when I was eight days old. As for the Law, I was a Pharisee; as for working for religion, I was a persecutor of the Church; as far as the Law can make you perfect, I was faultless. But because of Christ, I have come to consider all these advantages that I had as disadvantages. Not only that, but I believe nothing can happen that will outweigh the supreme advantage of knowing Christ Jesus my Lord. For him I have accepted the loss of everything and I look on everything as so much rubbish if only I can have Christ and be given a place in him. I am no longer trying for perfection by my own efforts, the perfection that comes from the Law, but I want only the perfection that comes through faith in Christ, and is from God and based on faith. All I want is to know Christ and the power of his resurrection and to share his sufferings by reproducing the pattern of his death. That is the way I can hope to take my place in the resurrection of the dead. Not that I have become perfect yet: I have not yet won, but I am still running, trying to capture the prize for which Christ Jesus captured me. I can assure you my brothers, I am far from thinking that I have already won. All I can say is that I forget the past and I strain ahead for what is still to come; I am racing for the finish, for the prize to which God calls us upward to receive in Christ Jesus. (Ph. 3:4-14)

In some sense all of us would like to know the future. At the same time, we are exceedingly frightened by the prospect.

However, searching for pattern in one's history is not aimed at foretelling the future. It is rather to help us understand the present so that we can respond more fully to God's love as it is moving us.

The Phase of Searching

The activity of searching is an attempt to discover in my own history a consistent manner in which God relates to me. It is a spiritual activity and so I pray to be enlightened about the continuous pattern of God's relationship with me throughout the mystery of my whole life. I am searching for a knowledge of a pattern that is my own and applies uniquely to my whole life.

Such knowledge requires God's revelation to me for it is not immediately clear. This is partly due to my lack of reflection and partly because the interrelationship of God with his creatures is hidden: "Now we are seeing a dim reflection in a mirror" (1 Co. 13:12). I turn in my searching to the revelation of God as given in the history of mankind. My chief source of insight as a Christian is the pattern of salvation history presented in the Old and New Testament. Like Jesus and the prophets, I look back over this sacred history to see the ways of God with human beings and from this platform discern his unique way of relating with me.

This means that two elements are important and intertwined in my searching. These are my own historical experience and the faith community's knowledge of God's relationship with persons in salvation history. I may begin by remembering my own life experiences and search out a pattern by comparing it to the accounts of God's activity in sacred scripture. Or, I may see in God's relationship with the persons of scripture a pattern that assists me in my searching.

The Pattern of Spiritual Growth

This phase concerns pattern as well as search. So it is important to indicate what is meant by the pattern of one's history. First, it does not mean a life experience that is predetermined by laws such as the pattern technologists might discover in their experiments with energy, chemistry, plants or animals. Second, it does not mean a static model like an architect's blueprints. And I do not want to suggest that history repeats itself, as the advocates of the "Eternal Return" might hold, for every moment in history is unique. The pattern of one's life experience I speak about is developing and evolving, living and personal. Yet, it has elements about it that suggest a manner, a repetition, a mode, a melody, a known way in which someone acts but acts freely.

It is possible to discover such an evolving and growing pattern in one's spiritual life. It is the same kind of pattern that is experienced in the interpersonal life between humans. When the psalmist says, "Yahweh is good, his love is everlasting, his faithfulness endures from age to age" (Ps. 100:5; *cf.* Ps. 119:137-140; Heb. 10:23), he is aware of the many ways God's love and faithfulness have repeatedly come. The pattern is not static but personal. There is always surprise and newness in God's pattern of love and faithfulness. "Now I am making the whole of creation new," Christ says in the Book of Revelation (Rv. 21:5).

The pattern is of such a nature that its outer limits and ramifications cannot be anticipated. God's infinite ways of relating to me cannot be known. The experience of love is always surprising. Yet, it is recognized as love. So, too, after the fact, a new experience of God's love will be recognized to fit the ever-expanding pattern.

The pattern will follow the living type we find in God's relationship with Israel, as well as that in the life of Jesus. In the Old Testament the pattern of relationship with God is presented by or through images. For example in the Old Testament God speaks to Israel in these words: "In the wilderness, too, you saw him; how Yahweh carried you, as a man carries his child, all along the road you travelled on the way to this place" (Dt. 1:31) "Does a woman forget her baby at the breast, or fail to cherish the son of her womb? Yet even if these forget, I will never forget you" (Is. 49:14,15). "For Yahweh is creating something new on earth: the woman sets out to find her husband" (Jr. 31:22). "When Israel was a child I loved him, and I called my son out of Egypt . . . I myself taught Ephraim to walk . . . I was like someone who lifts an infant close against his cheek; stooping down I gave him his food" (Ho. 11:1-5). Thus the pattern of God's relationship with Israel is that of God as father, mother and husband.

The evolving pattern of relationship between God and mankind is also suggested by the ongoing efforts of Yahweh to woo back Israel in the face of her hardheartedness. "That is why I am going to lure her and lead her out into the wilderness and speak to her heart" (Ho. 2:14,16). "I am going to renew my covenant with you; and you will learn that I am Yahweh, and so remember and be covered with shame, and in your confusion be reduced to silence, when I have pardoned you for all you have done" (Ez. 16:62,63). "I have been Yahweh, your God, since the day in the land of Egypt. I will make you live in tents again as on the day of Meeting" (Ho. 12:9, 10). "Israel, come back to Yahweh, your God; your iniquity was the cause of your downfall" (Ho. 14:2). God's faithfulness constantly adjusts to Israel, allowing the relationship to be a living, developing one.

A further understanding of the kind of pattern being considered in this phase is found in the human life of Jesus as a child, an adolescent, a carpenter, a rabbi, a companion and friend of apostles. "Do you understand," he said, "what I have done to you? You call me Master and Lord, and rightly; so I am. If I, then, the Lord and Master have washed your feet, you should wash each other's feet" (Jn. 13:13,14). "I call you friends, because I have made known to you everything I have learned from my Father" (Jn. 15:13-15). Jesus' human life is the pattern *par excellence* of our relationship with God. "For by His incarnation the Son of God has united Himself in some fashion with every man. He worked with human hands, He thought with a human mind, acted by human choice, and loved with a human heart. Born of the Virgin Mary, He has truly been made one of us. Like us in all things except sin" (*Vatican II*, pgs. 220-221).

Because he is son of God, he also demonstrates in his life with other human beings a further insight into what is meant by pattern. The symbols he uses of relationship to others are growthful and intimate. He is the vine, the apostles are the branches (*cf.* Jn. 15:1-17). Another symbol of his concern for others is that of a shepherd taking care of his sheep: "I am the good shepherd; I know my own and my own know me and I know the Father; and I lay down my life for my sheep" (Jn. 10:14,15). Thus, the attitude of Jesus indicates that God relates to human beings in an interpersonal way that is living, growing and serving.

Patterns in Sacred Scripture

Scripture indicates that there are four kinds of patterns in God's dealings with human beings. These can be classified as: 1. a general pattern in single events, 2. a general pattern in a person's whole life, 3. a unique pattern in single events, 4. a unique pattern in a person's whole life.

By general pattern in a person's whole life is meant those elements that are common to the whole lives of the great persons of scripture such as Abraham, Moses, Ruth, Isaiah, Judith, Jeremiah, Mary, Jesus, Paul. The general pattern in single events refers to the common elements these same persons would have in events such as their background, birth, upbringing or call from God. The unique pattern in a person's whole life is different from the common elements in the general pattern. For example, in Jesus' whole life, the unique pattern is present in the special elements of his suffering, death, and resurrection. The unique pattern in single events is the special element that shows up in a spiritual event, for example the blinding of Paul at the time of his conversion and call.

General Pattern in Single Events

The best examples of a general pattern in single events are the moments of call to different leaders. Thus, in the Old Testament, we see with Abram, Moses, Isaiah, Jeremiah, a general pattern when God calls them. The form is usually of this nature: God speaks a name (sometimes he gives a new name, for example, Abraham). God awaits an answer—a free response in faith. The person is set apart for a work God calls him to do. Finally, the person, often in fear and hesitation, accepts with an assurance that God will remain faithful although there is no guarantee of what will happen. (*cf.* Gn. 15:1; 17:1; 22:1; Ex. 3:4; 4:10-12; Is. 6:9; 62:2; Jer. 1:6,7,11; 20:7).

The New Testament presents a general movement in single activities and experiences of Jesus. Jesus' baptism, temptations in the desert, agony in the garden show a general pattern such as his humility as a man, hearing the Father's word and experiencing the pull of the Holy Spirit. He can even be filled with turmoil, confusion, or fear until he transcends himself in surrender and dependence on the Father. Similarly in his activity of preaching and healing there is a general pattern. Jesus' presence calls forth trust or hardheartedness. Trust leads to a declaration of forgiveness followed by healing (*cf.* Mk. 3:22-30), and hardheartedness to statements such as "You will die in your sins" (Jn. 8:21).

In the call of Peter (Jn. 1:42; Mt. 16:18) the pattern of the Old Testament is repeated. Peter's call comes in stages throughout the New Testament. He meets his call in Jesus. Peter's response is one of being overwhelmed by his sinfulness like Isaiah (*cf.* Lk. 5:1-11). His name is changed from Simon. Peter is set aside to be a fisher of men and finally to head the Church. A similar pattern is present in the conversion and call of Paul (Act. 9:1-30). All the elements of the pattern, however, may not be present in every call.

From such examples one can understand why the masters of the Christian spiritual life have written and spoken of certain single events of their lives, such as a vocation call or a prayer period in terms of a general pattern. There is the spiral of the spiritual journey classically expressed in the recurring experiences of purgation, illumination, union; purgation, illumination, union, etc. There is a pattern of affective responses when experiencing God's call—awe, confusion, unworthiness, humility, fear, surrender, openness to whatever is asked. There are rules for recognizing the patterns of temptation. There are dependable signs that indicate the presence of good or evil forces in a person.

General Pattern in a Person's Whole Life

The Book of Wisdom, chapters 10 to 19, refers to the long history of God's actions and the responses of the Israelites. It is possible that the prophets used the general pattern found in the overall history of God's dealings with Israel to support them in their discernment of events. The prophets themselves present the general pattern in terms of the allegory of a shepherd and his sheep, a vinegrower and his vine, or a man and his wife (*cf.* Ezek. 16). God is always faithful, leading Israel to more and more responsibility. Israel is constantly falling back, succumbing to the false gods and wealth of her pagan neighbours or following unwise leadership. Yet, there is a movement forward to a new covenant as Jeremiah says: "Deep within them I will plant my law, writing it on their hearts" (Jer. 31:33).

For the Israelites, the fact that God carried them through the desert "as a man carries his child, all along the road you travelled on the way to this place" (Dt. 1:31), recalls the basic pattern of Israel's history. It is beyond themselves; the experience of being sustained, called to freedom and taken further than they thought possible. They are sustained as slaves in Egypt, then called by Moses to trust in Yahweh, and next make the transcendent response to go out into a death-dealing desert, a fearful, unknown place of possible pain, starvation, and death. In the desert they sin and fall into a new slavery, but, even so, God sustains them in forgiveness, calls them anew, and they make further self-transcending responses. And this rhythm continues into the time of David and the prophets. The pattern repeats itself, but in a constant transcending movement forward in self-awareness as a people led by God.

The evangelists speak of Jesus as one who understood the Old Testament pattern much better than the scribes and pharisees and could use it to understand his own life. Sometimes what he says indicates that he saw his life and mission in terms of the general pattern of history found in the Old Testament. " 'Who do people say the Son of Man is?' And they said, 'Some say he is John the Baptist, some Elijah, and others Jeremiah or one of the prophets' " (Mt. 16:14). "This is a wicked generation; it is asking for a sign. The only sign it will be given is the sign of Jonah" (Lk. 11:29). "Jerusalem, Jerusalem, you that kill the prophets" (Lk. 13:34). From his prayerful reflection on the Old Testament, in terms of his own life, Jesus experienced his whole life as the movement of God's sustaining, calling, and transcending power. He was able to foresee his passion, death, and resurrection. He does so three times (Mk. 8:31; 9:31; 10:34). He could see himself as the "suffering servant" prophesized in Isaiah, the New Israel, alone and without a home: "foxes have holes and the birds of the air have nests, but the Son of Man has nowhere to lay his head" (Mt. 8:20). The evangelists also indicate that Jesus discerned when the general pattern of the prophets was expressing itself in his life. "My hour has not yet come," he could declare at Cana (Jn. 2:4). When the hour did come Jesus walked on ahead towards Jerusalem (Mk. 10:32).

After Jesus has lived the general pattern of his human relationship with the Father he reveals it in a more explicit manner after his resurrection during different appearances to his apostles. His appearance to the disciples on the way to Emmaus is a very clear description of one of these occasions. "You foolish men! So slow to believe the full message of the prophets! Was it not ordained that the Christ should suffer and so enter into his glory? Then, starting with Moses and going through all the prophets, he explained to them the passages throughout the scriptures that were about himself. Then they said to each other, 'Did not our hearts burn within us as he talked to us on the road and explained the scriptures to us?' " (Lk. 24:25-32).

Unique Pattern in Single Events

The experience in single events may pick up a pattern that is present in a person's whole life and give it further specification. David is a good example from the Old Testament. He was aware of the special place he had in God's eyes from the many times God had given him victory or protected him from his enemies. David's life has a pattern of this kind: humble station, challenge, victory, prominence. This is seen in examples from his life as a shepherd boy triumphing over Goliath, a young man being hunted by Saul and escaping, an adult tribal chieftain summoned to rule Israel. The incident of being confronted by Nathan with his sins of adultery and murder impressed upon David a new understanding of his humble state. The resulting death of his child, the later birth of Solomon, and God's forgiving him increased David's awareness that his prominence was God's gift.

The uniqueness of Jesus' own experience at single moments and throughout his earthly life appears in instances like his baptism where he heard the words: "This is my Son, the Beloved; my favour rests on him" (Mt. 3:17); or in his temptations in the desert where he experienced the temptation of being messiah: "If you are the Son of God?" (Mt. 4:3,6); or the incidents like that of power leaving him: "Immediately aware that power had gone out from him, Jesus turned around in the crowd and said, 'Who touched my clothes?' " (Mk. 5:30); or his surprise at those who received the message: "I bless you, Father, Lord of heaven and of earth, for hiding these things from the learned and the clever and revealing them to mere children" (Mt. 11:25). These would seem to be growth experiences for Christ as he became aware of his relationship with the Father. Each single event is unique, but they fit in with a pattern of Jesus' sense of humility, recognition by the Father, and experience of special power.

St. Paul speaks of his conversion experience in Galatians: "Then God, who had specially chosen me while I was still in my mother's womb, called me through his grace and chose to reveal his Son to me" (Ga. 1:16). More details of this experience are given in Acts (Ac. 9:1-9; 22:6-11; 26:12-18). Paul also speaks of other incidents of religious experience in a letter to the Corinthians where he describes himself as a person who was "caught up into paradise and heard things which must not and cannot be put into human language" (2 Co. 12:4). But in incidents of personal suffering Paul understands experiences as giving further insights into his own life: "For it is when I am weak that I am strong" (2 Co. 12:10). And so he desires "to know Christ and the power of his resurrection and to share his sufferings by reproducing the pattern of his death" (Ph. 3:10).

Unique Pattern Throughout One's Life

While there is a general pattern in God's dealings with human beings throughout the Old Testament as well as in the human life of Jesus, there is also a unique pattern that is present. We see this in the whole life of such persons as David, Jesus and Paul.

We might, in a study of the lives of Abraham, Moses, David, Judith, or the prophets of the Old Testament, discover a unique pattern of God's relationship to them throughout their lives which would be a clue in the phase of searching. David's humble status, his trust in the Lord in battle, his experience of persecution by Saul, his religious respect for God's anointed, his sins with Bethsheba, his humility before Nathan, his love for his rebellious son Absalom, can indicate a pattern to be studied and compared.

But the most revealing pattern of God's unique relationship with someone throughout his whole life is found in the person of Jesus. His resurrection highlights both the uniqueness and the pattern of his life. The pattern is present in his incarnation, life, death, resurrection and return to the Father. And because Jesus is "the Way, the Truth and the Life" (Jn. 14:6), this pattern of life is important for all humanity. Thus, Paul exhorts Christians to consider seriously the pattern of Jesus' life for themselves: "In your minds you must be the same as Christ Jesus: His state was divine, yet he did not cling to his equality with God but emptied himself to assume the condition of a slave, and became as men are; and being as all men are, he was humbler yet, even to accepting death, death on a cross. But God raised him high and gave him the name which is above all other names so that *all beings* in the heavens, on earth and in the underworld, *should bend the knee* at the name of Jesus and that every tongue should acclaim Jesus Christ as Lord, to the glory of God the Father" (Ph. 2:5-11). Jesus' life is not to be imitated on a one-to-one action level (Jesus did this, I will do this). But a prayerful consideration of the pattern of his life can give enlightenment and courage for one's own life.

Paul's reflections on his own life suggest the unique pattern: "I have come to consider all these advantages that I had as disadvantages" (Ph. 3:7). He advances a similar pattern to the Corinthians: "Take yourselves for instance, brothers, at the time when you were called: How many of you were wise in the ordinary sense of the word, how many were influential . . .

No, it was to shame the wise that God chose what is foolish by human reckoning, and to shame what is strong that he chose what is weak by human reckoning" (1 Co. 1:26,27).

Searching by Comparing with Scripture Patterns

When I begin to search for the pattern of God's relationship with me, I can do it in two ways. The first way is to use the knowledge of pattern I see in the Old and New Testaments to suggest incidents and methods of investigating my own life for pattern. The second way is to go more immediately to my own life experiences and look for the spiritual elements that are present.

The first way involves a comparison of certain important incidents in my own life or the whole range of my life with similar incidents of persons in the Old and New Testament, in particular, with those of Jesus' life. I could also search for the pattern of my relationship with God by comparing my life with that of the Church and her saints down the centuries. The advantage of using sacred scripture is that it is a small library of books and the inspired account of God's actions with humanity.

I can compare my experience of being called by the Lord with the general pattern of calls of the Old Testament leaders, or of Saints Peter and Paul. Entry into the mysteries of Jesus' baptism, temptations in the desert and agony in the garden may also facilitate my search for pattern in the calls of my life.

It is also possible to compare my whole life with the general pattern in the whole life of persons in the Old Testament, of Jesus, and of the apostles. This is particularly true if I see my life in comparison with the pattern of Jesus' paschal mystery.

Paul's special insights into the general pattern of Christ's life are found in several passages. The apostle recognizes that there is a transcending energy in the humility of Jesus by which his act of obedience overcomes the results of mankind's disobedience. "But however great the number of sins committed, grace was even greater" (Rm. 5:21). And so Paul prays to share in this general pattern: "All I want is to know Christ and the power of his resurrection and to share his sufferings by reproducing the pattern of his death'' (Ph. 3:10). And St. Paul did just this. This moves me to suspect that this pattern could be present in my own life as it was in his.

Paul is also aware that God's plan and desire is ''that we should become his adopted sons, through Jesus Christ'' (Eph. 1:5). The significance of adopted childhood in Christ tells me something about the general pattern of my own life in relationship to God.

Everyone moved by the Spirit is a son of God. The spirit you received is not the spirit of slaves bringing fear into your lives again; it is the spirit of sons, and it makes us cry out, 'Abba, Father!' The Spirit himself and our spirit bear united witness that we are children of God, and if we are children we are heirs as well: heirs of God and co-heirs with Christ, sharing his sufferings so as to share his glory.

. . . We know that by turning everything to their good God co-operates with all those who love him, with all those that he has called according to his purpose. They are the ones he chose especially long ago and intended to become true images of his Son, so that his Son might be the eldest of many brothers (Rm. 8:14-17,28,29).

This fact of adoption encourages me to search out the pattern of my life in terms of the pattern of the whole life of Jesus, the son of God. This method is in keeping with that of Jesus and Paul. They realized that scripture is the best commentary on scripture, and that all of scripture must be recalled. Jesus had the experience of Israel, her leaders and prophets, as a general pattern to understand his unique history. St. Paul, in turn, could add the general pattern of Jesus' life to those of the Old Testament for his search. I can use the general pattern of all three—the Old Testament, Jesus' life, and Paul's life, to discover the unique pattern of my relationship with God.

Unique Pattern in Single Events

Besides comparing one's life with the general pattern found in the Old and New Testaments over single events and a whole history, there is the prayerful investigation into the pattern that is unique to oneself. Again, these unique patterns can be studied in single events or throughout one's whole life.

There are many single events in my own life where I can detect a recognizable pattern of God's relationship to me. Some of these are moments of prayer, celebration, love, times of success or failure with friends, study, sport, music, and so forth. They are the times when God's presence or absence was noticed. Careful reflection over the experience of prayer and a new approach for reflecting on my daily experiences of life can put me in touch with these single events.

Maslow's work has given us a new appreciation and understanding of the single events he calls peak experiences. The new interest and practice of the discernment of spirits has also focused on such single events. Gradually a new willingness to accept the phenomenon of the movement of spirits has come into existence.

Through the consideration of single experiences a new type of knowledge and awareness of the interior relationship with God develops. I am able to get in touch more and more with the signs of my relationship. This includes all levels of my being, the biological, psychological and spiritual. I look at my spontaneous reactions on all three levels to judge the meaning of what is taking place. I judge whether God is present or absent in these interior movements by looking at my motivation and my actions.

Among the single events I may investigate are those of call, temptation, sin, virtue, desolation or consolation. I reflect upon the unique pattern of God's relationship to me through such moments. It is important to study the beginning, middle and end of such events where there has been a notable presence or absence of God in my life.

My own pattern of call is unique even though I may have compared for clarification the elements of my life leading to a vocation with the calls in the Old or New Testament: Isaiah, Jeremiah, Judith, Our Lady, Andrew, Peter, Matthew, Martha, Mary, Paul, Timothy. In reflection I may realize that the call began with an experience of success moving me from consolation to humility, then to offering myself to God. Or I may realize that the call began with failure, moving me from discouragement to crying out to the Lord, followed by indifference (spiritual freedom) and finally to a response to call. There will be many permutations and combinations of these variables. I need to reflect prayerfully to discover my own particular collection.

Similarly with temptation there may be a recognizable pattern in a single event. Does it begin with anger, frustration, depression (self-pity), fatigue (sensuality)? Does it begin with great insight, desires to do great things for God? Does it begin with consolation and move to recklessness? Does it begin with desolation and move to self-gratification? Some, like Paul, are more tempted in the exercise of zeal (strength): "as for working for religion, I was a persecutor of the Church" (Ph. 3:6). Some, like Peter, are more tempted through lack of religious motivation (unwillingness to suffer), insecurity, fear: "Peter, followed at a distance" (Lk. 22:55).

Another experience where there is a pattern to be detected is in my responses to grace. How this takes place is unique. Today, I may reflect on my name of grace, the beatitude which fits me, the article of the Creed that speaks to me, or upon other things of this nature. I may question the situation leading to my call, or to my conversion. Is it the awareness of the mire into which I have sunk? Is it hearing a prophet condemn this passing world? Is it the sense of emptiness in all my achievements? Again, a sense of helplessness in my anger and resentment may make me cry out for help, and with the aid of another believer I may be led back in memory to the instances of real or imagined rejection by parents or friends. With God's grace, a healing of memories takes place as I am able to forgive in the spirit of Jesus' words, "Be compassionate as your Father is compassionate. Do not judge, and you will not be judged yourself; do not condemn, and you will not be condemned yourselves; grant pardon and you will be pardoned" (Lk. 6:36,37). The single events are recalled, met and examined. The grace to forgive is sought.

There are also experiences, sometimes peak religious experiences, that have no pattern to them. They are unexpected.

But they are very significant. The situation, time and place of the event, in which they occur should be examined to see if there is something common in the experiences. They can help me discern the significance of other peak experiences. St. Ignatius makes this observation about such peak experiences,

When consolation is without previous cause, as was said, there can be no deception in it, since it can proceed from God our Lord only. But a spiritual person who has received such a consolation must consider it very attentively, and must cautiously distinguish the actual time of the consolation from the period which follows it. [*336*].

I can also study other single religious experiences within a prayer experience that leads to spiritual consolation or desolation. Then, the discerning of spirits is important in a time of consolation as well as a time of desolation. The movement that leads me to Jesus and the transcending of myself is as important as how I am deceived. Often, I find that my "bright lights" about an apostolate or new-found freedom in sexual matters lead me down the "garden path" to discouragement or sin. The practice of reflecting carefully over such a prayer experience can lead me to discover a pattern in the consolation or desolation experienced.

There is also spiritual consolation and desolation in events outside the time of prayer. For example, in studies, in work, in interpersonal relations, I may begin to experience myself as worthless or trapped. The very structures of bureaucracy in the university, political, and business worlds are experienced as depressing in some instances, and freeing in others. What is the pattern when I became closer to God or separated from him? What is the movement that strengthens my faith in this everyday life experience? What is the movement which weakens my faith?

When people investigate single events in their life for patterns they will discover certain elements and rhythms appearing over and over again. Each pattern is uniquely experienced by the person. The following are examples of such patterns.

The person could be moved from anxiety over responsibility and the question "Why me?" to a free experience "Why not me?"

The beginnings for another might involve a good inspiration, then joy, then fear, then uncertainty, doubt, struggle, then trust in God leading to peace.

A first experience could be a gentle nudge, then a call, then a challenge followed by interest, then fear of the pain and suffering involved, and finally the presence of the Lord who brings peace.

For another person, the first experience is fear, then a capitulation to God's plans.

Another might find that in the beginning there was a need for purification, then the motivation was elevated.

On the other hand, sympathetic persons might try to dissuade one from suffering for Christ.

Someone might experience enthusiasm for a cause, next tend to flounder and become aware of weakness, and then call on the Lord.

Another's progression would involve surprise, then fear, then inadequacy, then seeing the possibility of growth.

Unique Pattern in the Range of My Whole History

The activity for discovering the unique pattern of one's spiritual relationship with God in single events is a way of leading into the searching for the unique pattern of one's whole life. The pattern in single events tends to focus on isolated events or persons in one's life. The unique pattern of one's whole life includes the impact upon other people and reaches for more external knowledge. Yet, it is very personal and interior. This pattern will include all the integrating factors in one's whole life.

This search proceeds from my belief in the resurrection and in the presence of Jesus to his apostles after his death as he taught them still further and encouraged them. It is founded on a hope in the transcendence of my present limitations right now, with him by my side today as well as after death.

The pattern that is unique in a person's life-history is the one which keeps recurring. I discover that I not only sin, am forgiven, or respond to grace in single events, but that there is a continuing history of sinning, being forgiven, and responding to grace. I have a sin-history and a blest-history. My sin history is closely linked to my blest-history. The impact of my sinning and of my responding to grace, upon others besides myself also begins to be highlighted.

When I consider my sin-history I may become aware of an accompanying grace recurring with it. The implications of what I have put into movement can be overwhelming unless I see that the pattern of sin is immediately counterbalanced by the activity of grace meeting it. "But however great the number of sins committed, grace was even greater" (Rm. 5:20). Looking over the years I may see how God has been present at such times. Or I may discover a pattern in my sinning and rising from sin that is not only repetitive but developing. "You know me through and through, from having watched my bones take shape" (Ps. 139:15). God has been there helping me grow and develop spiritually as well as biologically.

The pattern discerned is not just one of being sustained and forgiven. I look for how I am not only a graced person, sustained and forgiven, but also an instrument of grace for others. I search for this pattern throughout my life. When has this been so in an ordinary way or in an extraordinary way, in a quiet experience or in an excruciating experience, in an experience of suffering or in one of celebration?

The perception of my sins and responses to grace which come together and the experience of myself as developing historically encourage me to investigate the pattern of my whole history without excluding certain parts I might fear or want to forget. The search for the pattern of my whole history now includes that of my sin history in terms of my blest-history which, in turn, includes forgiveness along with the history of myself as an instrument of grace for others.

This pattern is historical in that it is recognized as taking place over my whole life span and in the interpersonal context. I also recognize the developing element in the pattern of my instrumentality with God. But it remains mystery because I see how God has done the unexpected through me and will do the unexpected again. Still, I have a glimmer of what has been, is, and may be. As Paul puts it: "Now we are seeing a dim reflection in a mirror" (1 Co. 13:12).

I may investigate my whole life to pick out those single events in which I have discovered myself transcending my usual fears, sins, basic disorders, in some instances, even to anticipating an emptying-out of self as happened with Christ. In line with Paul's sentiment of Philippians 3:7, I may begin to recognize throughout my whole life that what I sought as advantages were empty and meaningless, and what I at first considered disadvantages were advantages for the building of Christ's kingdom. My very emotional and personal weakness can be used through Christ's love to make me an instrument of grace in helping someone else. The state of a person in weakness seeking help from another person who has and still may experience a similar weakness creates the healing community of love.

A general pattern of transcending can also be recognized when I look at the effect of my life upon other persons. I become aware that my own experience of sin and rising from sin is a witness to others and so I search for the unique pattern. I may begin to recognize a pattern of humility because of sin leading me to be sympathetic and compassionate with others. Or I may see a pattern between my own sinful fears and disinterestedness in the sufferings of others and the supportative effect of this human weakness to other people trying to do works of mercy. The others see the human weakness (sin, lack of patience, lack of compassion, etc.) in me, another apostle, and this highlights the transcending action of God who calls sinners to build his kingdom. I may become conscious that my weakness and cowardice sometimes expresses itself in outward strength which I don't necessarily feel interiorly. God draws good out of my evil. I may see tensions, confusions, desolations, conflict and even anger as part of the movement within community and within myself by which God brings forth his work. The words of Isaiah come back to me: "For my thoughts are not your thoughts, my ways are not your ways—it is Yahweh who speaks" (Is. 55:8).

I can reflect upon my life to discover the unique pattern of how I am God's instrument. For example, at times I experience myself caught in a weakening emotional situation. I do not feel in control of the situation, nor indifferent, nor cool and recollected. I feel sinful, limited, helpless, driven to possess something or someone. I experience all the contraries of the free, outgoing, pure, selfless person my vocation as a Christian calls me to be. Then in a conversation with someone else I experience being led beyond myself. The other person has had the same kind of experience and is reaching out to me for help, and amazingly I find that I can respond in concern and compassion. I notice that it is a pattern that keeps recurring through my life.

In some persons an almost frightening pattern may be discerned where one's extreme consciousness of unworthiness, lack of value, lack of faithfulness immediately precedes meeting someone else anguishing through the same kind of creaturely, sinful state. Have you ever been caught up in love or compassion for another person to the extent of suffering excruciating pain at your helplessness or your separation, and then met another in a similar state? Or have you been working through violent feelings of envy, anger or jealousy at another's talents, or authority, and then found yourself helping another trapped in the same feelings? Seeing the human weakness (sin, lack of patience, compassion etc.) in another apostle only highlights the transcending action of God who calls sinners to build his kingdom.

And the pattern is such that the experience of helping another in anguish and confusion does not ease your own anxiety and anguish at the time. Yet, in the moment of conversation or dialogue you are able to distance yourself from your own anguish, but now with a glimmer of hope, for the pattern prepares you to expect such sufferings since they are an aid to others. "When we are made to suffer, it is for your consolation and salvation" (2 Co. 1:6). Maybe, in our interiorly oriented world of today, this pattern is the way we are given the apostle's joy in having "had the honour of suffering humiliation for the sake of the name" (Act. 5:41).

Confirming Signs of True Pattern

Pattern is discovered in recurrent phenomena perceived in one's whole life relationship with God. The kind of evidence which indicates that a true pattern is being discovered combines the harmonizing of the scriptural patterns with the experiences of personal history. These experiences of my life include all the common ones experienced uniquely and the special ones that are experienced only by me, and no other, as far as I know. Among the common ones of a human being are birth, parents, school, adolescence, adulthood, friends, sufferings, successes, failures, joys, fears, loves, and hates. The special ones are religious experiences that are known explicitly and often from exterior phenomena, such as Moses had before the burning bush, or the apostles, with Jesus on the mountain of the transfiguration, or St. Paul, when he was knocked off his horse and blinded. I may have other religious experiences that are at least initially implicit because I experience a change of attitude within myself in terms of an increase of faith, hope, and love.

Another sign that a true pattern is being discovered is the indication that God's continual faithfulness is evident in the pattern. Ps. 103 is a good expression that God is constant and faithful throughout a person's whole life. Jesus says this faithful constancy is due to his Fatherly care for all human beings (*cf.* Lk. 12:22-30). So the pattern should contain the constancy of God's sustaining presence as redeemer and creator.

Another sign of true pattern is that it allows for God's freedom to act unexpectedly within the pattern itself. God's consolations are known as free gifts in the pattern. The pattern is such that it is open for further expressions of God's love. If the pattern indicates some form of constraint on God, these should be recognized as signs of falseness in the pattern.

If what is discovered includes elements of transcending oneself interiorly with ensuing freedom and humility, this will be a sign of true pattern. The unexpected movement out of self in compassion, gentleness, peace, etc., are part of a true pattern when they fit a growing sense of gratitude. The growth in gratitude indicates humility and brings with it spiritual freedom. The elements of humility and freedom are good signs.

Again, the element of the transcending action of God using one to be his instrument is an important sign of a true pattern. This element is the transcending action experienced through oneself to others. In retrospect, when such action takes place, it is always experienced as an amazing occurrence even though it fits a developing pattern.

Thus, the signs of true pattern are recurrence, harmony with scriptural patterns, experience of God's faithfulness, flexibility and openness to the unexpected transcendence, humility, being an instrument of God's grace. The discernment that accompanies this phase recognizes that in the ever new experience of God's faithful love there is a harmony with the previous elements of pattern discovered. When this is not so, it is a sign that the full pattern has not been discovered or that the present experience is not fully understood.

The phase of searching encounters consolation when I sense a correctness and completeness taking place within me. I recognize in my life all the elements of a true pattern. And I have the satisfaction of seeing that this pattern fits the myriad experiences of my life with God and gives me a sense of their meaning and value.

THE ROLE OF A SPIRITUAL DIRECTOR

The following comments are intended to help a director come to more fully developed principles in guiding others to search out the pattern of God's initiatives in their lives.

A. Searching as a human process

The director knows that every human being more or less reflects on his past in order to make some sense out of it. More reflective persons may do this less symbolically and more methodically; but nonetheless, there is a natural element to the activity of trying to find out the meaning and pattern of one's past.

B. Searching for pattern is important in itself

One can only be aware of the pattern of God's initiatives after the particular event is lived through. Seldom can one be aware of this pattern before or during the event itself. The director should encourage the heuristic, discovery element in the search, and assist the person to be open in the future to the significance of what is found. The innate desire to seek the true, the good, and the beautiful are forever operating in each person. Not only is the pattern of the relationship with the Lord growing but so is the search. The director helps the one being directed to realize that *searching in faith* is part of the christian experience.

C. Various levels of searching

First there is the level of searching out the actual pattern of one's past, i.e., those patterns recurring over and over again which most people experience. Then there is the level of understanding one or two particular events which symbolize the overall cycles of one's life. Then there is the level of searching out the understanding of these events in the light of faith. At this point a director can encourage the person to make comparisons with the patterns of life presented in the Old and New Testament, putting a final emphasis on how one is reliving the pattern of the life of Jesus.

D. Searching in the light of Jesus' life

As the one being directed becomes more attuned to the pattern of the individual events of his own life, the director encourages viewing these in the light of the individual events of Jesus' life. For example, in the light of the contemplation on the birth of Jesus, the one being directed can be instructed to discover the mystery element in one's own birth. In the light of the events surrounding Jesus' birth—the connection with the Roman census, the long journey to Bethlehem, the redemptive purpose of Jesus' birth—the person may be disposed to search out further aspects and meanings of one's own birth. Therefore the director helps one not only to discover how to imitate Jesus, by the actions of doing this or that, but further, to search out in the single events and the whole of one's history that which corresponds to the pattern of Jesus' life. In such contemplations the person is encouraged to seek out comparisons, to discover parallels, to look for the indications of being an adopted child.

E. The paschal mystery is the key model for searching out one's history

Since the paschal mystery is the method that God has chosen for the redemption of every person, this pattern is written into the personal salvation history of each one. The paschal mystery is the general norm against which one can compare the pattern of God's initiatives both in the single events of one's life and in one's history as a whole. St. Paul did this and re-evaluated his whole life: "Being a Hebrew of Hebrews and a Pharisee" Paul once considered great advantages. In his re-evaluation in Phil. 3:7 he came to see that they are to be seen as disadvantages. The director may encourage the one being directed to discover the same truth by pondering the own personal history in terms of the paschal mystery of Jesus.

EXERCISE
Searching in the Lord

Introduction

Now some of John's disciples had opened a discussion with a Jew about purification, so they went to John and said, "Rabbi, the man who was with you on the far side of the Jordan, the man to whom you bore witness, is baptizing now; and everyone is going to him." John replied: "A man can lay claim only to what is given him from heaven. You yourselves can bear me out: I said: I myself am not the Christ; I am the one who has been sent in front of him. The bride is only for the bridegroom; and yet the bridegroom's friend, who stands there and listens, is glad when he hears the bridegroom's voice. This same joy I feel, and now it is complete. He must grow greater, I must grow smaller. He who comes from above is above all others;

he who is born of the earth is earthly himself and speaks in an earthly way. He who comes from heaven bears witness to the things he has seen and heard, even if his testimony is not accepted; though all who do accept his testimony are attesting the truthfulness of God, since he whom God has sent speaks God's own words: God gives him the Spirit without reserve. The Father loves the Son and has entrusted everything to him. (Jn. 3:25-35)

John the Baptist knew himself to be the bridegroom's friend. He recognizes very clearly his role as the one who waits for and witnesses to the bridegroom. This role was given to him from above: "A man can lay claim only to what is given him from heaven." He was deeply aware of the unique call that came from God. As with John, so with every Christian, God dialogues in special ways.

Suggested Approaches

I ask the Lord to reveal to me the pattern of his special dialogue with me so that I can recognize what is given to me from above, and where he has increased and I have decreased.

I pray for freedom and light as I begin with those single events in my spiritual life that are outstanding. I consider the nature of each single event, how it began, how it developed, and how it ended. For example, I will reflect upon:

The presence of God in peak experiences of call and response.

The sense of separation from God in strong experiences of temptation and sin.

The experiences of transcending acts when I feel I have gone beyond myself in acts of kindness, love, understanding of another, in acts of generosity or of surrendering myself to another's plan.

New insights into the spiritual life—intimacy with God—such as the awareness that in my weakness and failure the kingdom of Christ has been built; or Paul's experience that what I considered as advantages, I now see as disadvantages.

Then I look to see if there is a pattern, mode, rhythm in these single events.

Next, I move to my whole life's history, looking to see if the pattern in single events is present or enlarged, or if it is totally different. I can do this by comparing my life story with the scriptural patterns of the Old and New Testament, given in this chapter under the two headings, General Patterns, in the following way:

> I search through my sin history. Is there a pattern of sinful effects on others?
>
> I search through my blest history. Is there a pattern of graceful effects on others?
>
> I seek an indication of development or growth in the relationship between my sin and blest history.
>
> I examine the external elements of my life, my apostolate, to see the presence of God's activity and the pattern of my being used as a partner in God's salvific plan.
>
> I think of other topics, questions, ways of learning which reveal more intimately the pattern of God's dialogue with me. Here, the times I have been surprised to be an instrument of grace might help. What led up to the moment? What followed? It may be the center of a circular movement. Is there a larger cycle repeating itself? Do I see an unique but growing spiral effect? Do I find my life to be similar to that of Paul or Peter? Thomas or John? Martha or Mary? Is it out of my failures and weaknesses that I find God present and using me? Is it out of my strengths and successes? Where does the transcendence of God's grace usually appear?

Finally, I consider the pattern I am discovering to see if the signs of a true pattern are present and I wait for the consolation that it fits my life relationship with God to arise.

7 THE PHASE OF WHOLENESS

They came to a small estate called Gethsemane, and Jesus said to his disciples, "Stay here while I pray." Then he took Peter and James and John with him. And a sudden fear came over him, and great distress. And he said to them, "My soul is sorrowful to the point of death. Wait here, and keep awake." And going on a little further he threw himself on the ground and prayed that, if it were possible, this hour might pass him by. "Abba (Father)!" he said, "Everything is possible for you. Take this cup away from me. But let it be as you, not I, would have it." He came back and found them sleeping, and he said to Peter, "Simon, are you asleep? Had you not the strength to keep awake one hour? You should be awake, and praying not to be put to the test. The spirit is willing, but the flesh is weak." Again he went away and prayed, saying the same words. And once more he came back and found them sleeping, their eyes were so heavy; and they could find no answer for him. He came back a third time and said to them, "You can sleep on now and take your rest. It is all over. The hour has come. Now the Son of Man is to be betrayed into the hands of sinners. Get up! Let us go! My betrayer is close at hand already." (Mk. 14:32-42)

I begin this chapter with the above quotation from the New Testament because I think it expresses very dramatically the wholeness our Lord sought and experienced as he began his passion. What his life experience was and where it was going was excruciatingly present to him. To labor through all this and to be obedient to the will of his Father required a sense of wholeness. And so, he prayed, "saying the same words" until he understood and could go forward in peace to his crucifixion and death.

The third phase in the activity of appropriating one's history in faith is wholeness. Again, this phase is related to the first, second and fourth phases. The two preceding phases of remembering my life's history and of searching for the pattern in it can be considered as preliminary to the actual appropriation, whereas, the third phase of wholeness and the fourth phase of openness are more directly appropriation. The initial instructions to recall my sins by a special effort of the memory, and to recall the blessings given by God our Lord are disposing the person to prepare for the gift of our Lord; so this third phase picks up the preliminaries of remembering and searching the past, and moves to an appropriation that is more concerned with the present.

The further appropriation of my history as it affects the future takes place in the fourth phase, openness. This is similar to those directions where a retreatant is asked to investigate the pattern of temptation discovered through particular experiences as a help for the future. When I have had such an experience and reflected upon it, I am able to guard myself against this type of deceit from the enemy.

The phase of wholeness has the dimensions of activity and affectivity. The activity is the exercise of taking responsibility for my past. The affectivity is the sense of wholeness experienced by the person during the activity. This affective experience is a sign that appropriation in faith is taking place.

I may perform some spiritual exercises to encourage this phase to begin or to develop. These exercises will present me with the desire and method of taking responsibility for my past. Then the consolation that is experienced when this phase of faith appropriation is taking place is the affective experience of wholeness.

The Activity

The basic activity in this third phase is that of taking responsibility for my whole life.

Taking responsibility for my past should be understood in terms of the word "response". This is not to claim that I have initiated all the elements in my life. It means that I responded to them. When I take responsibility for my past, it means that I see a personal dimension in everything. Incidents which others might not consider personal or only environmental I see as part of my spiritual relationship with God. This applies to positive and negative life experiences with God. It includes sinful and virtuous acts. I take responsibility as a free person responding to initiatives of God in graceful acts or in rejecting God's initiatives by sinful acts.

The account of Jesus' birth and life afford an example that everything in my life's history is for me whether I like it or not, and in that sense, all is filled with the presence of God. This means everything is for my spiritual growth and spiritual relationship with God. Such questions in the gospel as, " From Nazareth? Can anything good come from that place?" (Jn. 1:46) might suggest questions raised in the mind of Jesus, as well as in the minds of the apostles. How did he see the fact of his birth? How did he accept his destiny of death on a cross? I have suggested that Jesus was able to take responsibility for his life by meditating on the Old Testament, especially on the Suffering Servant Songs of Isaiah (Is. 40:1-55:13). I should add that Jesus did not have a martyr complex with respect to his rejection, suffering, and death, but rather a joy in knowing his life was in conformity—with the love of the Father for mankind.

Jesus was able to be obedient unto death as we see in the garden of Gethsemane, " 'Abba (Father)!' he said 'Everything is possible for you. Take this cup away from me. But let it be as you, not I, would have it' " (Mk. 14:36). Again, on the cross, he says, "Father, into your hands I commit my spirit" (Lk. 23:46).

How do I take responsibility in faith for my past? It is a grace from the Lord. However, as in any other spiritual activity, I can prepare myself by entering into this spiritual dynamic, and by seeking the grace to have the perspective of responsibility for my whole life.

This activity as a development of the previous two phases involves remembering my past history and searching for the pattern of my relationship with God. Now, I enter upon a further awareness that the grace-filled, sin-filled history is my own. Even the elements over which I have had no control as, for example, my parents, the time and place of my birth, the genes that give me my intellectual ability, personality, talents, and so forth, are my own, and God our Lord has been present in all this from the beginning. Similarly, God has been with me while I was rejecting his love (sinning) or showing initiative and strength before a challenge. All these are mine.

As I am reflecting over myself in this history I can become angry, discouraged, non-believing. I may think of myself as a haphazard occurrence, or a pawn of nature, or a plaything of a cruel God. Or I may discover that I am angry with the Father over the circumstances of my life. I may feel bitter, alienated and resentful.

A help in this activity is to pray over the life experiences of Jesus. As I contemplate Jesus on the cross and consider certain questions or as I remember the movement in Jesus' life from his birth on, I may gain insights into my own history. I may tend to neglect certain parts of my history where I have been hurt, failed or sinned. When I consider Christ's sufferings a sense of fellowship with him may arise.

How is it that though He is the Creator, He has stooped to become man, and to pass from eternal life to death here in time, that thus he might die for our sins. . . . What have I done for Christ? What am I doing for Christ? What ought I to do for Christ? [*53*].

. . . what they are doing, for example, making the journey and labouring that our Lord might be born in extreme poverty, and that after many labors, after hunger, thirst, heat, and cold, after insults and outrages, He might die on the cross, and all this for me. [*116*].

Such prayer might allow me to take responsibility for my life without any pretensions to grandeur or martyrdom. I may experience a sense of wholeness through my history.

The Affectivity

The activity of taking responsibility is accompanied by a sense of wholeness. What is this affective experience of wholeness that I am to recognize? How can it be described? Whence does it arise?

Wholeness is a true spiritual consolation given by the Holy Spirit. It begins as I experience a harmony in my being between the events of my life's history and the pattern of my relationship with God which I have been seeking through reflective prayer.

The sense of wholeness will be experienced differently at different moments in the appropriating of my life-history. Continuing discernment of this wholeness and spiritual direction is needed, as I remember my life and search for the pattern of relationship with God. The continuing inter-relationship of these three phases is part of the adventure that is the spiritual life.

As I search the events of my life in faith, I am forced to meet my history and begin to respond to it. As a pattern emerges in searching out the revelation of God's continual relationship to me in all that I have done and in all that has happened to me, acceptance is made easier. My history takes on a new meaning, and I recall further events of my life which fill in the pattern that I am discovering. Already in the activity of recalling and searching out a pattern there can be the beginnings of wholeness. At this point there may be a sense of well-being in hope, that is, there may be a quiet expectation that I will find meaning and understanding which fits my life experience.

After the remembering and searching, the activity of taking responsibility for my life gives me further opportunity for this growing sense of wholeness. As this grows I can look for certain aspects of wholeness to help me recognize whether or not the growth is authentic. These aspects are the experience of exigency, meaning, acceptance, identity, continuum and humility.

Exigency is that active, interior desire to discover a spiritual pattern in my life and to seek responsibility in it. The desire is a peaceful one for it comes from faith and is experienced as a call to a deeper understanding of my dialogue with God leading to a further union with him in the future. I am aware of this exigency not only as I begin the process of searching for the pattern of my life with God, but also when it remains and continues to operate as the pattern clarifies itself, and as I become conscious of my responsibility. The continuing desire to know more and more about this covenant love which God has for me and the human race and to accept it positively is an aspect of wholeness. It is part of the dynamic involved in the relationship with God throughout my history.

It can be said that meaning is known in the light of faith, because I am a mystery to myself. Yet, my faith says that my life is meaningful and not absurd. My faith says God is the source of meaning because God is the source of freedom, realized especially in the free man, Jesus Christ (*cf.* Jn. 1:18; 8:36). A further aspect, therefore, in the process of appropriation is the meaningfulness that I discover as I search out the pattern of my life's history and seek to be responsible in it. More and more of my life takes on meaning as God reveals more and more about my life and his relationship to me in it. When I fail to find the meaning of my life, I know that I am not enlightened and so I continue to search for meaning.

Again, this sense of meaning that I have attained in searching and seeking to be responsible has to be part of an open dynamic. The pattern I discover cannot be closed because I know that God is always capable of doing the unexpected. Even when I have perceived his manner of inviting me and of my response, I will always experience it as unexpected. As love acts received from a familiar lover are always delightful and surprising, I find a delightful surprise in the movements of God's love for me.

Acceptance in this growing sense of wholeness concerns myself and my actions as a responsible person. This is not to be confused with discovering my responsibility for sinful and virtuous acts, as I do in an examination of conscience. Nor is it the activity of taking responsibility for my whole life's history. What is experienced or felt is a result of exercising myself to take responsibility for all of my past, that which I like and do not like.

Again, if the sense of meaningfulness in my life history is

seeing God's loving designs in my life, then the seeking of responsibility can rise to the positive feeling of acceptance in this dialogue with God. Wholeness is experienced when in confusion, I accept my history as part of me, and when in humility I also accept that I have responded to God's urgings in my heart and actions (my blest-history). Such response is an adult act.

Acceptance is present as I look at my history and am able to face both the sinful and graceful dimensions of myself as an historical, free person. I accept joyfully this responsibility now, and I see how my historical moments alone and in company with others form my response to God's relationship with me. This sense of acceptance means that I am in touch with the social and cultural dimensions of my history, whereas, previously I felt only anger or unconcern. My life is response to all this, for God is present and I accept. With Dag Hammarskjöld I can say: "For all that has been—Thanks! To all that shall be—Yes!" (*Markings*, Alfred A. Knopf, New York, 1969, pg. 89). Now, I see my history as drawing me more and more into a corporate sense of acceptance. (*Cf. Vatican II* pgs. 260-261).

But the acceptance is my own. It is possible because I have hope in God's salvific desire for me as St. John has declared: "Yes, God loved the world so much that he gave his only Son, so that everyone who believes in him may not be lost but may have eternal life" (Jn. 3:16). It is an element in the experience of wholeness for it relates to my personal history. It directs me backward to Christ's salvific act for me and forward to my future responsible acts with him.

Identity is a further aspect in the phase of being whole. I know myself as unique before God and other persons. I experience this uniqueness when I reflect upon the influences which fashioned me (my parents, culture, religious upbringing). Even though I have been subject to much the same life experiences as others, I know myself as unique. My love for myself and what I discover keeps growing.

Identity may also be described as honesty with self. I may know myself as perplexed, ambivalent and divided. There are many tensions in my being arising from the basic fears of creaturehood and sinfulness or from psychological experiences of relationship with persons in the past. But an awareness develops that God has not only been present to these tensions but is working through them to build his kingdom. The insights into the pattern of my relationship with God help me to find identity and to experience wholeness.

This identity is not one of passivity or quietism; awareness and acceptance of responsibility continues. There is an inner demand to work for the kingdom. So the perplexity about myself, the uncertainty about what to do and how to gain the strength to do it, may remain at the same time that I am sensing identity. This experience is the dynamic one of being sustained in meaningfulness and love as my life moves forward.

Continuum may be a part of this sense of identity that I experience. I do continue to exist. The investigation into pattern and responsibility gives me a sense of union with God I did not have before. It is a sense of continuity in time as well as in space. I can find here my relationship with ancestors, the Church, Jesus Christ. I can also realize my continuity with the cultural and social values that have influenced my life.

Continuum is also an awareness that the determining elements of my physical, social, and cultural past have not been the only influence on my life. Freedom has been at work in me. I am aware of God's presence carrying me beyond these influences. So my sense of history and continuum is experienced as a dynamic union in God with other people of history down the years.

The increase of humility that comes to me with this awareness of grace and freedom confirms my wholeness. It is a love of self that is not pride or self-centeredness. It is one of open expectancy to the Lord's goodness. I can recite my own *Magnificat* with Our Lady.

As I come in touch with the pattern of my responsible relationship with God, I am caught up in wonder. Humility gives rise to compassion towards myself, forgiveness for myself, and a sense of humor with myself. It accepts my weakness, my limitation and sinfulness as well as those of others in the whole historical setting of my life. This applies to my ancestors, my country and my church. Patience attests that humility is achieved wholly—"As for Mary, she treasured all these things and pondered them in her heart" (Lk. 2:19).

Discerning the True Sense of Wholeness

When I am appropriating my history in faith as well as in other activities leading to authentic decisions, the danger of deception is always present. "It is the mark of the evil spirit to assume the appearance of an angel of light" [332], *cf.* 2 Co. 11:14). Therefore, the question of whether the sense of wholeness is a true or false consolation is important. How do I discern true from false? There are deceptive and true experiences of wholeness. The deceptive experiences tend to avoid responsibility for the past and the future, or to absorb me with the present. True experiences accept the element of responsibility in the past experiences of failure and success while facing the future in hope.

Sensual gratification, as well as an attitude of non-involvement, may give me experiences that feel complete for the moment. But these are deceptions. A fatalistic attitude to life may give me a feeling of peace and control. I may approach my history with the attitude that God is in total control and that my part is just to exist. Quietism is such an expression of this totally passive resignation to life. Fatalism and quietism lack the active response to God's initiative of love to me, and so they give a deceptive sense of wholeness.

Besides these deceptive senses of wholeness, there are legitimate experiences of it that are different from the consolation of spiritual wholeness attained through the activity of appropriating my history in faith. This spiritual wholeness is more than the positive peace that might come from a kind of psychological realism. This psychological peace is the acceptance of my past as past and now out of my control with expressions such as "What's past is past!" or "That's the way I am!" It is a peace that is necessary at times for psychological well-being to face the future. Spiritual consolation comes from insight into the Lord's pattern of relationship with me. It is the consolation of recognizing the dynamic or growth pattern of my spiritual relationship with God as it moves me from the past into the future.

The sense of wholeness is more than the positive experience of well-being within myself that results from a feeling of identity with the cosmos. Such is the kind of well-being I experience with nature, for example, at the seashore on a sunny day with the sound of the surf in my ears. Another example of this might be my experience of music or of an athletic achievement whose gracefulness and beauty fill my whole being.

There is also a contentment that comes with passive resignation to the will of God whatever comes. It is a type of holy indifference. But the sense of wholeness from the appropriation of my history in faith is more than this, because there is a meaning and hope discovered that makes my history and its future direction more acceptable.

Again, the sense of spiritual wholeness is different than those legitimate experiences of pleasure such as come from food, drink, sex, or achievement. It is more than the instances of spiritual peace that might come to me from the experience of forgiveness when receiving absolution during the sacrament of reconciliation.

This sense of consolation from spiritual wholeness catches up my whole history and does not reside in momentary experiences. I am able to discern in this wholeness a grasp of my history that includes the dimensions of sorrow for sin, fear of suffering, hope of salvation. I know my sins, sufferings, and failures of the past as permeated by the continual presence of God. My past experience and history point to the future. I know how God has been with me through all these experiences. This wholeness does not express itself in unrealistic resolutions. I am truly conscious of my sinful tendencies and find hope in God's faithfulness to his promises, promises I find already fulfilled in the pattern of my history.

This sense of wholeness is dynamic and not static. I do not feel "I've got it made." Rather, I know that there are many elements in life and in the social milieu that exclude this kind of absolute certainty. Thus I know that I am not in a position to totally control my life or my future. But this sense of wholeness fills me with the certainty that is hope, "and this hope is not deceptive because the love of God has been poured into our hearts by the Holy Spirit which has been given us" (Rm. 5:5).

This sense of wholeness also expresses itself in my prayers for light and strength as I realize that the pattern of my past reveals the future demands to be faced. I am not passive before the future but attempt to meet it in prayer. The consolation of discovering a pattern does not remove the awareness of freedom and responsibility; rather, it reveals the opposite. It increases the freedom and responsibility which I accept in this phase. An old spiritual maxim applies here when in darkness and weakness I accept my responsibility: "Pray as if it all depends on me. Leave the success of the venture to God."

The sense of wholeness should be honest and truthful. My negatives and disorders—these will remain present. Cowardice, fear, passion that blinds and debilitates will also remain. But the hope that comes from the presence of God in the past can move me to pray for bravery, strength, and the light of love and reason. Although God has worked in spite of and through my faults I am not to become complacent or to continue in sin. As Paul says, "Does it follow that we should remain in sin so as to let grace have greater scope? Of course not. We are dead to sin, so how can we continue to live in it?" (Rm. 6:1,2). I may continue to be an obstacle to God's grace but hopefully in a different way. The polarity of opposites in me that are part of my history will not disappear.

A further testing of the true sense of wholeness is the experience of freedom and detachment that I have as I see my life converging more and more with the life of Christ. I am consoled by finding the presence of spiritual poverty, actual poverty, humiliations and rejections in the pattern of my own history, and I can look ahead for repetitions of the same (*cf.* 2 Co. 1:3-7). In fact the acceptance of these past experiences can help and allow me to make the kind of prayer suggested by St. Ignatius in these words:

. . . the grace to be received under Christ's standard, first in the highest spiritual poverty, and should the Divine Majesty be

pleased thereby, and deign to choose and accept me, even in actual poverty; secondly, in bearing insults and wrongs, thereby to imitate Him better.

It will be very helpful in order to overcome the inordinate attachment, even though corrupt nature rebel against it, to beg our Lord in the colloquies to choose us to serve Him in actual poverty. We should insist that we desire it, beg for it, plead for it.

. . . in order to imitate and be in reality more like Christ our Lord, I desire and choose poverty with Christ poor, rather than riches; insults with Christ loaded with them, rather than honors; I desire to be accounted as worthless and a fool for Christ, rather than to be esteemed as wise and prudent in this world. So Christ was treated before me. [*147, 157, 165*].

The phase of wholeness will include evidence from beyond my person. It includes the social dimensions of my failures and my insensitivity to others; the sense of my inadequacy, smallness and frustration; as well as my successes, compassion, magnanimity, and co-operation. Thus it is not passive or static but active and alive. It expresses itself in my acceptance of others (as well as myself) in their limited, sinful, developing history and in my wish to co-operate with them to build up the kingdom here on earth.

A certain realism is present in this wholeness. My memory of the past and the pattern that I have discovered give me spiritual insight into who I am before God. This appropriation now becomes data that will help me in further decision-making with God. The fact that it is known does not remove the affective and emotional dimensions of my history or even of the recall of my history. In fact, I should know that I will often react similarly in the future. But hopefully, the appropriation of my historical relationship with God will help me to see more quickly the relevance of God's guiding action with me. It will help me recognize more quickly both the more crass and the more subtle deceptions of my enemy.

Thus wholeness is found when my history fills me with hope for the future. This appropriation will carry with it the sense of humility and the desire to be with Christ. Humility and desire will once again be signs of the true consolation of wholeness. I seek more and more to be obedient to the call of God as I experience this consolation in individual instances, and as I recognize it in the pattern of my unique life with God.

A Growing Experience

Because the appropriation of my history in faith is an evolving activity, the sense of wholeness is a growing experience. While it develops or is promoted, three aspects are important and should be continually discerned. These are the existential data of my life, the comparison of my history with all the mysteries of Christ's life, the movement forward in humility and generosity.

As I consider the pattern of my relationship with God and take responsibility for my life, the sense of wholeness should continue to fit the interior and exterior events I recall. A kind of reciprocal action takes place of testing the sense of wholeness with the style of my history being discovered and *vice versa*. I realize that I need to return often in prayer to the data of my life experience. I know that this kind of reflective prayer keeps returning to the events and to the pattern of my experience in much the same way as I am to consider further prayer periods: "In doing this we should pay attention to and dwell upon those points in which we have experienced greater consolation or desolation, or greater spiritual appreciation" [62]. The growing sense of wholeness is the consolation present in me accompanied by spiritual appreciation of the pattern of my life relationship with God.

When testing and promoting the ongoing experience of wholeness, comparison with the mysteries of Christ's life as given in scripture is important. Further appropriation is possible when I compare the pattern of my own life with that of Jesus' life. This comparison throws light on the pattern I may be discovering, and it may give a further sense of wholeness. I am to discern both the aspects of insight and affectivity as the process continues in relationship to Christ's life.

To see the pattern of suffering and rising in my own life

helps me to accept the possibility of future suffering and to anticipate it as Jesus did: "Now we are going up to Jerusalem, and the Son of Man is about to be handed over to the chief priests and the scribes. They will condemn him to death and will hand him over to the pagans who will mock him and spit at him and scourge him and put him to death; and after three days he will rise again" (Mk. 10:33,34). In appropriating this aspect, I have seen those transcendent dimensions of being drawn by God's grace through weakness, failure, and suffering to strength, success, and well-being in the style of my own life, and I am able to enter the future in terms of the suffering, death and resurrection of Jesus. I am able to discover in my own unique life that there are parallels with the emptying out (*kenosis*) of Christ in the incarnation (the acceptance of self) and in the garden of Gethsemane (the acceptance of the Father's will for me in the human condition). I should also see that there are experiences of the resurrection (self-transcendence) in the pattern of my life.

When, in contemplating the mysteries of Christ's life, I seek the grace of "an intimate knowledge of our Lord, who has become man for me, that I may love Him more and follow Him more closely" [104], I may come to the realization that I have been following Christ in his history even if only in a limping fashion, and thus I may experience the consolation of wholeness. Or I may ask Jesus to reveal himself to me as he is present in my very history, and in this revelation I may experience such consolation.

The realistic way in which I face the future is a sign that I am appropriating my history. Part of this realism is a willingness to go beyond my natural fears and capabilities. To reflect upon my own historical experience within the context of the Church's experience and Christ's experience can be the moment when this willingness is born to me. Such a gift from the Holy Spirit is a sign of wholeness. This realism involves the transcendent desire to die with Christ. Searching into the pattern of my life with God lends encouragement for me since this kind of dying has already been part of my historical life. Reflection can bring this fact into the light. The acceptance now, of past sufferings and humiliations can be a spiritual experience of union with Christ.

By reflecting on my history, I have already been making the passage through death to life. I know that I have already experienced in my own life the passion of Jesus and rising with him. So I am enabled by this grace of insight to surrender myself to the further paschal experiences which my life may hold in store. Therefore, I may realize that "I am suffering now, and in my own body to do what I can to make up all that has still to be undergone by Christ for the sake of his body, the Church" (Col. 1:24).

Often in a prolonged prayer experience over a decision, I discern that there is in my past a pattern of transcendence. In the light of my desire to be poor with Christ poor, insulted and accounted a fool for Christ, I may realize with reflection and direction that the difficult experience of praying over my sinful past life earlier in the retreat has given me a sense of my own spiritual poverty and rejection in Christ. This is so, even when I have been the cause of my own experience of rejection. It may mean that I have gone through the purifying experience of repentance and sorrow for my sins out of love of Christ. Such an awareness of transcendence helps me to face the future realistically.

I may now recall other past experiences of embarrassment and humiliation for Christ and these may help me to appropriate my whole history, and enable me to face the future possibility of dying in Christ, yet surviving in love. When the sense of wholeness is present, I know my pain and discouragement in terms of the sufferings of Christ. When there is an accompanying hope and desire to suffer in the future, my sense of consolation is true; I am not indulging in self-pity, but am truly humble before the Lord.

When I see the comparison between the pattern of my own life and that of the life of Jesus, the effort to be an instrument joined to God (*instrumentum conjunctum cum Deo*) is helpful. The appropriation of my history in faith is both a sign and an effect of the desire to be such an instrument. It is also important that I see where and when I have been an instrument of God's grace for others in my life's history. I have been such an instrument when I have prayed for others or have given myself to others in the spiritual and corporal works of mercy. I appropriate my history more completely when I ask, "How can I be a better instrument for God?" Then the further question becomes necessary, "What does my history say to me?"

Thus, I might ask these questions: When was I mortified? When did my prayer go well? What was the situation out of which an apostolate arose? Which external movements have helped the Church in faith and love? What are the signs of holy discontent rather than those of an anxiety?

So, during this third phase, I become aware of the dynamic activity within—memory, search, wholeness—memory, search, wholeness—memory, search, wholeness. This prepares me for the next step that is suggested in the pattern of my life up to now—the phase of being open to this pattern's forward direction into the future.

THE ROLE OF THE SPIRITUAL DIRECTOR

The following comments are intended to help a spiritual director come to more fully developed principles in guiding others through the phase of wholeness. The role of the director here is to recognize the presence of the phase of wholeness beginning to emerge in the one being directed, to encourage this person to proceed with certain exercises to gain the sense of wholeness, and to help in the discernment of a true sense of wholeness from a false one.

A. Encouraging responsibility

The spiritual director will continually explain the stance of responsibility that one should assume, encouraging the person to take an existential view of life and to assume responsibility for it.

B. Experience of Jesus is a paradigm

As the sense of wholeness is emerging, the director can suggest that Christ's experience is a paradigm. Certain passages and incidents in the gospel presentation of Jesus, where there is an indication of growth, surprise, joy, and development in Jesus' own experience of himself, can be pointed out. This sense of wholeness will probably coincide with the experiences of the person whether of exigency, meaning, acceptance, identity, continuum or humility. These affective/cognitive reactions the director notices and he leads the one being directed to notice.

C. Discerning the true sense of wholeness

To help the one being directed discern a true sense of wholeness from a false one, the director will recognize the forward direction implied in such an affective experience. So, the director listens and affirms when the sense of wholeness being experienced is one that is open to this forward direction. Is the element of realism present? Does the nuance of spiritual hope ring true? Is there a desire to suffer with Christ?

The director also tries to recognize the false kind of peace or wholeness that comes from a form of fatalism concerning one's history. False peace has no sense of freedom or hope. Another type of false peace or wholeness can be a form of quietism, a form of passivism in which one opts out of responsibility for one's life. Another form of false peace is more subtle and carries with it a kind of presumption that masquerades as hope and freedom.

In this activity of seeking wholeness, the director is also listening for a false sense of humility. Thus the statement, "I can't do anything for the kingdom of Christ" can be an expression of true or false humility. It is false when some aspect of a martyr complex is present; it is true humility when one recognizes one's whole life as united with Jesus, and looks forward to building the kingdom with Jesus. A further sign of true humility is present when a person, accepting his or her own life history, still desires to go forward and to suffer with Christ in joy.

D. A Reported Experience

The following is an account of someone's prayer over her life's history and is printed with permission. As a young girl she had suffered through the depression and drought of a poor family. The affective experiences reported here contain aspects of a growing sense of wholeness.

After asking for the grace to appropriate my history in faith, I felt constrained to stay with the Lord. He seemed to indicate that he wanted me to stay in his presence, rather than have me call up events in my life. The feeling of being drawn to him intensified. There was no dialogue, no exchange, simply a sense of deep presence, intense peacefulness and joy at being together. At one point, however, he intimated that he is the beginning and the end of my history, that he lovingly designed generations of ancestors to bring me into life, that all comes from him and flows back to him. This period of loving presence continued for perhaps an hour or more. No recollections, no reminiscences of any kind occurred.

Suddenly from nowhere a childhood scene flicked on. As a child on the family farm I was standing in the middle of a waving field of golden wheat. The wind blew the wheat like an ocean of gentle tides, ebbing and flowing, under a blue sky with puffy, white clouds. This scene lasted but moments. There was no message, only the scene. The sense of gentle presence continued.

A second childhood scene turned on sometime later. I was in the school cafeteria, eating homemade bread that had been spread with a mixture of cream and Karo syrup. Again the scene lasted only seconds, followed again by silence for a few minutes. Then came the softly spoken words, "I have fed you with milk and honey." Strong sentiments of love and gratitude welled up in me for his tender care. A period of silence followed.

Suddenly, a third childhood scene flashed into my memory. I was coming up the gravel road toward home, could smell the baking bread. As I entered the kitchen, I saw again the many loaves of plump, golden bread. For a few minutes there was silence again. Then came the Lord's voice once more, "I have filled you with the best of wheat." Waves of gratitude, love flooded over me. He seemed to enrobe me with himself.

EXERCISE

Seeking the sense of wholeness that is my history

Introduction

Near the cross of Jesus stood his mother and his mother's sister, Mary the wife of Clopas, and Mary of Magdala. Seeing his mother and the disciple he loved standing near her, Jesus said to his mother, "Woman, this is your son." Then to the disciple he said, "This is your mother." And from that moment the disciple made a place for her in his home.

After this, Jesus knew that everything had now been completed, and to fulfill the scripture perfectly he said: "I am thirsty." A jar full of vinegar stood there, so putting a sponge soaked in the vinegar on a hyssop stick they held it up to his mouth. After Jesus had taken the vinegar he said, "It is accomplished"; and bowing his head he gave up his spirit. (Jn. 19:25-30)

Behind Jesus' words "It is accomplished," there is the experience of wholeness. This was not an isolated event in the unique history of Jesus, but another moment that gathered up his past and carried with it the sense of wholeness as his life came to completion.

Suggested Approaches

I ask the Lord to experience as a result of remembering and searching over my life's history the sense of wholeness that is my life.

I pray for the courage that is freeing as I search through my life to find the elements of Christ's call and activity throughout it. I seek faith and hope in the searching so that I will take responsibility for this life that is mine. So I ask myself, "When have I rejected God's call to me? When have I been obedient to that call?"

I will be able to do this only with Jesus, and so I compare my life and my desires to those of Jesus who realized that it was the Spirit of the Trinity that made it possible for him to be obedient in his responsibility. "The Father and I are one" (Jn.

10:30). "My aim is to do . . . the will of him who sent me" (Jn. 5:30). "My food is to do the will of the one who sent me and to complete his work" (Jn. 4:34). "The Father loves me, because I lay down my life in order to take it up again . . . and this is the command I have been given by my Father" (Jn. 10:17-18). "Father, the hour has come: glorify your Son so that your Son may glorify you; . . . I have glorified you on earth and finished the work that you gave me to do" (Jn. 17:1,4).

When I see the direction of my life's history with God and the forward movement that is there, I seek from the Lord peace, trust, and wholeness from my historical past to carry me into the future in hope and obedience.

8 THE PHASE OF OPENNESS

After saying this, what can we add? With God on our side who can be against us? Since God did not spare his own Son, but gave him up to benefit us all, we may be certain after such a gift, that he will not refuse anything he can give. Could anyone accuse those that God has chosen? When God acquits, could anyone condemn? Could Christ Jesus? No! He not only died for us–he rose from the dead, and there at God's right hand he stands and pleads for us.

Nothing therefore can come between us and the love of Christ, even if we are troubled or worried, or being persecuted, or lacking food or clothes, or being threatened or even attacked. As scripture promised: For your sake we are being massacred daily and reckoned as sheep for the slaughter. These are the trials through which we triumph, by the power of him who loved us.

For I am certain of this: neither death nor life, no angel, no prince, nothing that exists, nothing still to come, not any power, or height or depth, nor any created thing, can ever come between us and the love of God made visible in Christ Jesus our Lord. (Rm. 8:31-39)

Openness is the attitude of mind and heart that freely observes and follows the forward direction I perceive in my history. It is a further experience of consolation and is a gift from God. Openness is part of the movement of appropriating one's life in faith. It faces the future at the same time that it is conscious of the past. In fact, as the other phases of remembering, searching, and being whole are operating, awareness is growing that there is a direction in the forward movement of one's intimate life history with God.

As this awareness surfaces, it is more and more a sign of appropriation. I may then tend to back off in fear from the activity of appropriating my life in faith, or I can allow myself to be opened up to the forward direction I am discovering in the pattern of my dialogue with God. Often my experience is one of reacting in fear at first and then moving to an acceptance of the direction I am to follow.

In the process of appropriation, while I am remembering and searching and becoming whole, I am becoming open at the same time. But my openness takes on different expression and intensity as my situation varies. I may need healing or be on the point of conversion; I may desire to be generous with God or be faced with a decision. Any of these states will call forth my openness in its own way.

When I am open, the experience of God's active love tends towards trust, and I freely surrender myself up to the transcendent movement in my life which takes the form of being led in a certain way and direction. The experience is considered transcendent for both the being led and the effect in me are beyond my capabilities. For example, despite my own inadequacy in an apostolic task, I experience success, or I am crushed by human sorrow and yet I feel strength and joy in Christ. I become involved in a further reflection on the pattern of my life; to appropriate it more fully I ponder how God leads me continually. This means that I investigate the pattern of my life from a desire to be open to its implications in the future. I am willing to use the spiritual insights of my past experiences of being led. The more pressing a decision is, the more possible it makes the phase of openness as I appropriate my history in faith.

In the phase of searching I find the pattern of how God relates to me personally. In this pattern I may also recognize a forward direction in my history. Affective touch with this forward direction in my life will help me make correct decisions. The phase of openness allows me to investigate my life to find this forward direction and encourages me to go with this direction in my future decisions.

The open attitude of a person moving toward this appropriation will include the elements of freedom, commitment, desire and obedience. The presence of these elements helps me to recognize when I am in this phase of faith-appropriation and gives me light on how to move with it.

Discovering the Forward Direction of One's Life

There are two sets of spiritual experience which express openness to the forward direction in one's life. Both sets involve authentic decisions. One set is the special experiences of vocation or apostolic call and response to them. The second set is the openness experienced when everyday decisions are made in the Lord.

At such moments, by intuition or reasoning, I am in harmony with the relationship God has had with me during my history. And at such times I have been open to the forward direction that is present in my history and have experienced the elements of freedom, commitment, desire, and obedience. The more I assimilate this affective knowledge, the better I will recognize and be able to use it in the future.

I begin this study by considering how God has led me in certain incidents and decisions in the past. When did I make correct decisions? When incorrect? What was the pattern of feelings? What was the pattern of exterior events? What helps me discover the forward direction of my life with God?

Many decisions in early years and youth have to do with the ideals of Christian living. They are concerned with temptation and sin. Of course, this effort continues throughout life. The larger decisions that effect one's pattern of life such as the choice of friends, profession, university, job, spouse, location of livelihood, or vocation, can be touchstones for examining and appropriating the forward direction of the call central to one's life.

Once again, an initial openness is necessary as I search for the direction in my life. Looking back I can judge which decisions I made concerning my life. Where have these been good, where bad? I may become aware of how seldom I have really made decisions. Most of the time I have fallen into situations. Again, I may be surprised at the presence and patience of God with me.

Am I willing to admit openly that some of my decisions are made in terms of God's desire but many are not? Yet, God is present. Now looking back at these decisions in terms of their movement towards God, I may get an insight into the consolation arising from my history as I recognize there a pattern of making good decisions. I may also get an understanding of desolation from my history as I recognize the pattern leading me to bad decisions. The act of remembering helps me to discover the direction of my life and to recognize the experience of openness.

The willingness to recall my history of decision-making can give rise to a spiritual knowledge that will help in the future. I may come to know what is the true consolation that indicates the forward direction of my life by studying the good decisions made in the Lord. Similarly I may come to recognize the desolation indicating a false direction.

First, it is important to discover when and where I have made significant decisions. Some of them may be as basic as resisting temptation or yielding to it. Others will concern my way and manner of life.

Next, I should categorize these decisions as good or bad. This is more easily done when I am aware of the pattern of my life history with God. Correct decisions can usually be discerned from their fruits. Good results will be indicated when I am more charitable, more concerned about God and others, more at ease in living the Christian life, more influential to others for good. St. Paul gives this list: "What the Spirit brings is very different: love, joy, peace, patience, kindness, goodness, trustfulness, gentleness and self-control. . . . We must stop being conceited, provocative and envious" (Ga. 5:22, 26).

Third, I should study how the decision was made. What was the situation? How did the question arise? What were the natural and spiritual results of the decision? What effect has it had on my ongoing life?

The next step is to look within myself for the interior direction or forward movement that is present in the good decisions. It is important to consider the different affective states in these correct decision-making experiences. When and how did hope or fear arise? Did the decision come out of suffering and loneliness, or out of joy and fulfillment? How did the resolution to go forward with the decision come about?

Correct decisions, that is, decisions made in union with God, can be made in suffering or in joy. Decisions made while suffering may show a forward direction, and so may those made while in joy. Is there a commonality? When did there come awareness beyond the suffering and beyond the joy? Besides helping me to discover the forward direction in my life, this awareness will say something about my future affective experiences with God that indicate the openness needed in future decisions.

Among these correct decisions are some that show most emphatically the forward direction and give the affective experience of openness. These are the special spiritual experiences which indicate a call from God to a way of life or a new apostolate. They can be the paradigm of correct decisions and should be studied most carefully on all levels of one's historical experience—biological, psychological, sociological and spiritual. When and how did the call originate? How did it develop? What were my interior feelings? What were the external effects? How do I know that my response was correct? Finally, when I compare such calls in my life, do I perceive a forward direction in my life and do I recognize the affective state of openness?

Forward Direction in Sacred Scripture

There is a forward direction in the history of Israel's covenant with God. This forward direction Jesus recognizes as paralleled in his own life and he carries it forward. St. Paul in turn recognizes the forward direction in Jesus' life; in fact, he sees his own life as a continuation of Jesus' (*cf.* Col. 1:24). With Paul the Church extends Jesus' continuation of covenant-history until the end of time. I study the forward direction of the Old Testament, Jesus' life, Paul's life, the Church's history, and my community's history, and I compare my history with these other histories to discover the forward direction of my own life.

The thesis that God reveals himself to mankind in the forward direction of history is well attested. A special example of this revelation is the chosen people. Moses and the prophets were given discerning powers to recognize the forward direction in Israel's history. They understood this history as a self communication of God and of his desires for this people.

I begin by comparing the forward direction of my history with that of other persons of faith and test my sense of openness. In the Old Testament the pattern of direction is best seen in the calls of God to individuals and the nation: God speaks a name (*cf.* Gn. 15:1; Ex. 3:4; Jr. 1:11); God gives a new name and proposes a mission (*cf.* Gn. 17:5; 32:29; Is, 62:2); God awaits a response in faith and freedom (*cf.* Ex. 4:10-12; Jr. 1:6); God achieves through history what he had promised but in such an unexpected way that only reflection upon history can recognize the direction (*cf.* Is. 55:8,9; Rm. 5:15-21). It is present as mystery (*cf.* Eph. 1:9). A similar pattern of direction is present with God's call to his chosen people, Israel, especially in covenant relationship (*cf.* Ex. 19:3-8).

The Old Testament is the relationship of God to Israel. It is God's plan of salvation worked out in history. God has a goal for Israel and the forward direction brings it about. The direction includes the election of the patriarchs, a promise of posterity and land, a fulfillment of the promise through the historical events of the exodus from Egypt, the covenant at the Mount Sinai, the conquest of Canaan, and a future eschatological kingdom with God. The prophets and the psalms continually speak of God's plan (*cf.* Ps. 33, 77, 78, 105, 106). They interpret historical events by pointing to the goal of God's plan. This goal is the salvation of all nations and the redemption of sinners. For example, the prophet Ezekiel recognizes the direction of Israel's future by the pattern of past events. Ezekiel understands that Yahweh's love for his adulterous bride, Israel, will continue into the future, "I will remember the covenant I made with you, when you were a girl, and I will conclude a covenant with you that shall last forever" (Ez. 16:60,61).

The basic forward direction is that given in the life of

Jesus. The forward direction contained in the calls in the Old Testament anticipate that of Jesus who completes them. The life direction of the saints and of the Church are patterned on that of Jesus (*cf.* Col. 1:24; Ga. 2:20; Ph. 3:11).

Jesus sees himself as sent by the Father (*cf.* Jn. 6:57; 20:21). He presents himself as the climax of the preparatory period that went before him: "Since John the Baptist came, up to this present time, the kingdom of heaven has been subjected to violence and the violent are taking it by storm. Because it was towards John that all the prophecies of the prophets and of the Law were leading" (Mt. 11:12,13; *cf.* Lk. 16:16). This leads to the question: What forward direction can be seen in the Old Testament leading up to the event that is Jesus?

The history of Jesus fulfills and interprets the law and the prophets of the Old Testament in a new and forward way. The gospel writers present Jesus as another Abraham, Moses, David, prophet, savior of his people (*cf.* Mt. 1:21; Lk. 1:32; Mt. 16:13-20; Jn. 5:45-47; Jn. 8:54-58).

Jesus interprets his life in keeping with the plan of God. He is sent by the Father (*cf.* Jn. 6:57; 10:36). He obeys by coming into the world of mankind (*cf.* Jn. 9:39; Mt. 5:17). He fulfills his Father's will (*cf.* Jn. 4:34; 6:38). His passion and death are a necessary part of this plan (*cf.* Mk. 8:31; Jn. 12:34). His preaching and miracles are signs that the kingdom is at hand (*cf.* Mt. 12:28). What he is, says, and does expresses the forward direction of the Old Testament (*cf.* Lk. 4:17-21; 22:37; 24:7,26,44; Jn. 13:18; 17:12). In his understanding of God's plan he can prophesy the stages of his life that pick up the direction of the Old Testament and continue it beyond expectations. Compare "Choose life, then, so that you and your descendants may live in the love of Yahweh your God" (Dt. 30:19) with "If anyone wants to be a follower of mine, let him renounce himself and take up his cross every day and follow me. For anyone who wants to save his life will lose it; but anyone who loses his life for my sake, that man will save it" (Lk. 9:21-24). In the movement of life-death-resurrection-glory, he reveals the secret of accepting suffering and dying. There is a new period between fullness and the end of time in which we in the Church now participate. He is able to proclaim a more growing and spiritual model of life to us as he anticipates his resurrection.

The application of the general movement of Jesus' life for ourselves and its importance for a future direction is made by St. Paul in the early church (*cf.* Ac. 2:23; 4:28; 1 Co. 15:3). In Romans, Paul sets out another large pattern: predestined, called, justified, glorified (*cf.* Rm. 8:28-30). Paul sees that, in the mysterious ways of God, disobedient mankind has been redeemed because of the disobedience of Israel who rejected the Christ, but who in turn will be redeemed from their disobedience (*cf.* Rm. 11:30-32).

Paul does not limit himself to the theological problem of the history of Israel. He is able to take the concrete historical condition of the Corinthians and relate it to the style of Christ's life: "Here we are preaching a crucified Christ . . . For God's foolishness is wiser than human wisdom, and God's weakness is stronger than human strength" (1 Co. 1:22-25). In his own life he can see the same movement and thus willingly desire its future direction: "To stop me from getting too proud I was given a thorn in the flesh . . . I pleaded with the Lord three times for it to leave me, but he has said, 'My grace is enough for you: my power is at its best in weakness'. . . . and that is why I am quite content with my weaknesses, and with insults, hardships, persecutions, and the agonies I go through for Christ's sake. For it is when I am weak that I am strong" (2 Co. 12:7-10). In his own life and that of the Corinthians, Paul seeks a pattern whose forward direction is correct because it fits the life of Christ.

The prophets, Jesus, and Paul see that the future is already at work in the past and the present. (*cf.* Jr. 44:29,30; 17:1-4; Ez. 20:4,5; Mt. 13:14,15; 16:2,21-23; 26:31-34, 54-56; Jn. 12:37-40; Rm. 11:1-6). They do not read the mind of God in a miraculous way. They read history and men's hearts (*cf.* 1 Kg. 3:9, 25-28; Mt. 12:25-28). Knowing from the past that God is a saviour, they prophesy not only a restoration but a new covenant (*cf.* Jr. 31:31-34; Lk. 6:35,36; 22:19,20; Jn. 3:17; Rm. 8:3).

Jesus and the prophets are aware of an overall historical movement. God calls mankind to be a partner in a covenant for building the kingdom. Mankind rejects this call and covenant and says no to God. Still God continues to save, and his saving act is always beyond expectation: "However great the number of sins committed, grace was even greater" (Rm. 5:12-21). Further on in the New Testament, Paul understands that the call to be a Christian will follow the way of Jesus' life which is humiliation, obedience, death, resurrection and glory (*cf.* Ph. 2:1-12).

As I continue to make comparisons, my perceptions develop. If I consider the possible forward direction in my history in juxtaposition with that of the pattern in scripture, I derive new insights and conceive more questions for discernment and more need of openness. The repetition of the activity of comparing continues until, in a sense of openness, I recognize the forward direction in the pattern of my life.

When I compare the pattern of my own life with the larger plan of God's salvific action in the Old and New Testaments does the unique direction of my life stand out? I may ask myself, "Has God given me a new name, a mission?" Do I see a forward direction of mankind, the Church, my community, that I am participating in? Am I interiorly free to investigate my pattern for its forward direction? Do I see a goal appearing in the beginnings and continuings of my life? Can I commit myself to this goal? Do I know it is unique in its relationship with Christ? Am I filled with hope and desire to go forward in the pattern of Christ's life as it has already appeared in my own (*cf.* Rm. 5:1-11; Eph. 3:14-22; Ph. 3:10-13)? Will I be obedient to this direction? Can I consider my crosses as good signs (*cf.* Ga. 6:14-17)? Do I consider that my sufferings for others are more valuable than the successes and pleasures that I myself have gained (*cf.* Col. 1:24; [53, 197])?

Now in a further openness I can look at my family tree. I can recall the state of my grandparents and parents and the situation of my conception and birth. Is there a sign for me in how God related to and prepared my parents? Do I see unique elements of directions here? What about the situation of my babyhood and early years? Can I see a forward direction in the presence of God in these years? The earlier and later teenage years can be very devastating and filled with idealism and guilt. Even though the memory is painful, yet I look back in hope. Are any persons (parents, friends, teachers, priests, sisters) the occasion for special awareness of God's call for me? In later years, in my work, profession, or state of life, do I continue to see a direction? How does the continuity of my life express itself in terms of direction? Can I see the elements of the plan of God? Am I willing to compare my life to Christ's? Does my life fit the pattern of Christ's: humiliation, death, rising? Can I face a similar movement into the future?

The forward direction in my life has an interior history of its own in which psychological understanding of myself is very important. It also has an exterior history and here the sociological model is helpful. While all my life-history is experienced personally, still in the appropriation of my history I am attempting to find the true way in which God relates to me and how he leads me. I seek the pattern of my dialogue with him and the direction that can be observed in that communication with him.

All of my past, including the psychological character of my ancestors and parents and the interior ways in which I responded to the social environment in which I grew up, is important in recognizing the forward direction of my life. But the external circumstances of my life should also be included as part of my search. What was the social environment of my past, the rank of my parents in the community, the position of the Catholic Church in my country? Where did I stand in the presence of my fellow human beings, for example, at home, in school, in sports, with those of the opposite sex?

Then there is a further search whose base is spiritual. My search for the forward direction in this history also has an interior and exterior dimension. Some signs of direction in my life are experienced interiorly, as when I am compassionate or self-forgetful or generous. The exterior signs of direction are the pattern of spiritual changes that take place in other persons, or in the social situation, or in an apostolate.

As I study the pattern of my life I seek out the real signs of direction in this history. The phase of openness requires a return to searching, but this time for signs of forward direction. The larger pattern, therefore, must be prayed over. I am seeking the positive direction that is present along with, or beyond, my personality traits. A study of the history of my virtues as well as my vices might be the beginning of this search. The awareness of my predominant virtue or fault or both can help in this investigation. But what I am seeking is sometimes only discovered by a kind of peripheral vision. It is the sense of positive movement in my life with God, whatever the beginnings, as operating throughout my life's pattern.

This is different again from the particular awareness of virtues or faults of the daily examination of conscience and the consideration of my progress over a week or a month. Generally speaking, such an examination is concerned about the particular actions one performs and not with the signs of development that might indicate a forward direction. In the phase of openness, however we are more concerned with understanding the development into the future.

The reflection on the forward direction of one's history includes a study of one's social impact on other human beings. When has such impact been destructive? When has it been creative? When has the impetus of God been present in this social history?

In looking for a forward direction in my history I should look at those passages through sufferings to joy, through failure to success, through selfishness to altruism. This history is further appropriated when these movements are accepted as indicative of direction into the future. Then, the investigation can go deeper. The purpose of this deeper investigation is to perceive the presence of true spiritual consolation in this forward direction of my life. This consolation helps me be open in the future when I wish to make correct decisions with God.

The pattern of forward direction in one's history includes peak religious experiences. Upon reflection these are seen to highlight the direction contained in the pattern of one's relationship with God throughout one's history. Peak religious experiences may confirm the pattern of relationship with God or indicate quite emphatically the forward direction that is present in the pattern of one's past life.

The very activity of looking for such a forward direction requires an openness to the future and at the same time creates an openness in faith. Faith shows me only a smudged image as at twilight time. "We are seeing a dim reflection in a mirror; but then we shall be seeing face to face" (1 Co. 13:12).

The Affective Experience of Openness

While the activity of perceiving the forward direction in one's history is proceeding, the consolation of the phase of openness may be happening. Here the elements of freedom, commitment, desire and obedience in one's own life are important, and I try to recognize the presence of these affective elements while discovering the forward direction of my life.

Freedom as a consoling element in the phase of openness is a sense of freedom with respect to the future as distinct from the sense of freedom with respect to the past. The freedom of accepting the past is present through the appropriation that has already taken place in coming to wholeness. In appropriating one's past history a trust in God develops from recognizing how God's presence has drawn me beyond myself to others even through pain and humiliations. This spiritual insight is freeing. I am given a realistic hope in God which opens me to the future. It encourages me to investigate the pattern of my life and sees its implications for the future.

Achieving openness to the forward direction being discovered involves gaining a prior freedom while searching for the pattern and a further freedom to accept the forward direction discerned. These two freedoms come together as an openness to the direction of one's history is gained.

The second consoling element in openness is commitment. Commitment in terms of openness can be described as an active state of readiness to follow the direction found in the pattern that is being revealed. The insight into the transcendent action of God's grace in the past can stir up the commitment of self to the growing possibilities flowing from the pattern discovered and appropriated. I experience a willingness to say "Yes" to the forward direction I perceive.

The third consoling element, desire, is similar to the second but with a slight nuance. I desire to make a decision with the Lord as I am caught up in the pattern I notice in my life with God. This picks up the insistence of Vatican II that we humans are responsible for the state of the world and our history is an expression of this responsibility. I experience a joyful anticipation of responding to the direction of my life and not a stoic resignation to what I must do.

The fourth consoling element is obedience. This is an obedience to the direction or movement of the pattern already observed. It takes effect when I surrender myself with love to the relationship with God which I have perceived. I stand ready to obey the direction that may reveal itself to a more careful investigation of the pattern in my past history. I open myself to this movement into the future.

This openness to the future flows from the insight of how God is transforming my heart. It is a result of the appropriation of my past in the state of wholeness described in Chapter 7. The awareness of freedom, commitment, desire, and obedience indicate an experience of God's continuing intimacy with me. They describe my affective stance towards the future. I acknowledge how I have been led in my past history, and therefore I accept the forward direction in this history. In generosity I wish to response to this forward direction that is contained in my history.

In this appropriation of my history in terms of openness to the future, I am aware that the history that I am appropriating is not static or mathematical. The pattern of my relationship with God throughout my life is dynamic. I may see the repetitive elements in the pattern; yet it is constantly new; as St. John says, "Now I am making the whole of creation new" (Rv. 21:5). By studying the pattern of my life with God I may see a direction and a way in which God leads me into the future. "In the wilderness, too, you saw him: how Yahweh carried you, as a man carries his child, all along the road you travelled on the way to this place" (Dt. 1:31). This awareness gives me trust and hope. I am opened to accept the direction I find in my past as it pertains to the future.

Remembering when I have been loved by God in the past

together with the insight of how this has taken place in my history helps me to develop a trust of God in the present. This trust is expressed in attitudes of freedom, commitment and desire towards the forward direction discerned. It enables me to be obedient to the future implications contained in my history. This surrender of myself in hope helps me to recognize even more clearly the forward direction in the unexpected events of my life and to respond by making better decisions born of confidence and openness.

The consolation of spiritual insight is the recognition of a forward direction in my history that I wish to pursue. The openness and acceptance of the implications contained in this direction is a further experience of consolation coming in this phase of the appropriation of my history in faith.

By this phase of appropriation, I recognize the direction in which God is leading me through my history. It also means that I acknowledge the significance of this direction for my future and freely commit myself to it with obedience and desire. This may be done in fear and trembling as I anticipate the implications for the future. But, having experienced God's continual forgiving and uplifting love before, I continue to hope.

In the making of correct decisions the willingness to follow Jesus into the future is the required consolation of openness for decisions in the Lord. The classical expressions of "indifference", "the imitation of Christ—poor and insulted", desiring "to do the greater thing" for God indicate the consolation of willingness that is needed. When the forward direction in the pattern of my history is part of my prayer, the decision will be a more thorough and convincing experience.

THE ROLE OF THE SPIRITUAL DIRECTOR

The following is intended to help a spiritual director come to more fully developed principles in guiding others through the phase of being open.

A. *Waiting for readiness and encouraging discovery*

When the spiritual director observes that the person

shows a readiness to investigate the forward direction in one's life the phase of openness is present. At this point the director encourages the one being directed to do the remembering and searching necessary to discover the direction in this personal history.

The director suggests that the person being directed return to the times of decisions and study the forward direction in them very carefully. The one being directed will know which decisions have been dominant, for example, a decision to leave home or a vocation decision or a job decision, and will begin there.

B. Being sensitive to the other person's response

After the director has made the above suggestions, sensitivity to the other person's response is important. Is there an eagerness to do this searching? Is there a willingness to follow the call-direction that the one being directed is becoming aware of? The consoling signs which indicate the degree of openness and progress in appropriating one's history are: freedom, commitment, desire, and obedience. These four signs confirm and test each other. The director is to be sensitive to them and discern the openness of the person and the significance of the forward direction being discovered.

C. Sign of freedom

The director watches for a freedom that comes from a trust in God's desire for the person. This trust flows from the knowledge of God's goodness and care in the past direction of one's life. It is a freedom that moves into the future without any debilitating fear. Yet it is not a freedom that comes from feeling one's own strength or control over the future.

D. Sign of commitment

The director looks for a commitment that is based on hope for the future and not on discouragement. There is a quietness about this commitment and not that of rash or boastful confidence. Commitment here is expressed by a readiness to follow the forward direction of one's life as it is continually uncovered by searching.

E. Sign of desire

The sign of true desire becomes evident when the director observes in the person a willingness to follow the lead of the Spirit as found in one's history. There is no hint of a grudging attitude or of a martyr complex; rather, this desire has the element of hope and expectation.

F. Sign of obedience

Obedience to the forward direction is basically a willing surrender to the transcendent element of call and direction observed in one's life history. This willing surrender is not a fatalistic succumbing to force. The obedience is not a flight from the direction discovered nor a fight against one's history. It is a sign of openness to the significance of one's history for the future.

EXERCISE

Hoping to become open to the forward direction contained in my history

Introduction

After the meal Jesus said to Simon Peter, "Simon, son of John, do you love me more than these others do?" He answered, "Yes, Lord, you know I love you." Jesus said to him, "Feed my lambs." A second time he said to him, "Simon, son of John, do you love me?" He replied, "Yes Lord, you know I love you." Jesus said to him, "Look after my sheep." Then he said to him a third time, "Simon, son of John, do you love me?" Peter was upset that he asked him the third time, "Do you love me?" and said, "Lord, you know everything; you know I love you." Jesus said to him, "Feed my sheep."

"I tell you most solemnly, when you were young you put on your own belt and walked where you liked; but when you grow old you will stretch out your hands, and somebody else will put a belt around you and take you where you would rather not go."

In these words he indicated the kind of death by which Peter would give glory to God. After this he said, "Follow me." (Jn. 21:15-19)

Peter was filled with memories of the past weeks. But he also must have remembered his first encounters with Jesus and all the events of intimacy, of failure, of suffering that he lived through with Jesus. These memories became the means by which he was prepared for the gift of openness and by which he became ready to hear the injunction: "Feed my sheep. . . . Follow me."

Suggested Approaches

I ask the Lord for the grace to be willing to look back on my life and to be open to following the forward direction as revealed in the intimacy of my life with God.

With hope I seek openness by remembering how the Lord has brought me through sins, failures, difficulties, sufferings in the past to a sense of redemption and value (wholeness). I seek openness by considering when and how I made good decisions in my following of Christ. I look back to see the beginnings of my vocation and the forward movement as it developed. I recognize how the Lord achieved his desire through me as an instrument in spite of my interference.

I can do this by comparing the forward direction in the pattern of my life to one of the saints of the Church, for example, St. Peter. I consider his call in Luke 5:1-11; his preaching and healings in Luke 9:1-6; his profession of faith and being scandalized in Mark 8:27-33; being prayed for by Jesus in Luke 22:31-34; his triple denials in Luke 22:54-62; experiencing Jesus' appearance to him in Luke 24:34; his triple profession of faith in John 21:15-19; his preaching and healings in Acts.

I ask to be open to the implications for the future in the pattern of my intimate life with God that I find in my own history.

9 CONSOLATION DURING DECISIONS AND EMERGENCE

When Jesus came to the region of Caesarea Philippi he put this question to his disciples, "Who do people say the Son of Man is?" And they said, "Some say he is John The Baptist, some Elijah, and others Jeremiah or one of the prophets." "But you," he said, "who do you say I am?" Then Simon Peter spoke up, "You are the Christ," he said, "the Son of the living God." Jesus replied, "Simon son of Jonah, you are a happy man! Because it was not flesh and blood that revealed this to you but my Father in heaven . . ."

From that time Jesus began to make it clear to his disciples that he was destined to go to Jerusalem and suffer grievously at the hands of the elders and chief priests and scribes, to be put to death and to be raised up on the third day. Then, taking him aside, Peter started to remonstrate with him. "Heaven preserve you, Lord"; he said, "this must not happen to you." But he turned and said to Peter, "Get behind me, Satan! You are an obstacle in my path, because the way you think is not God's way but man's."

Then Jesus said to his disciples, "If anyone wants to be a follower of mine, let him renounce himself and take up his cross and follow me. For anyone who wants to save his life will lose it; but anyone who loses his life for my sake will find it. What, then, will a man gain if he wins the whole world and ruins his life? Or what has a man to offer in exchange for his life? (Mt. 16:13-26)

The Consolation of One's History and Making Decisions

The affective state of spiritual consolation can be defined as a sense of union with God and a desire to love and serve him in return with all one's heart, mind, and body—in sufferings or in joys. The spiritual consolation of one's history involves a heightened awareness of this union and desire, which have, however, been present and operative throughout one's life. This consolation brings with it a continuous sense of existing as an adopted child of God.

Recognition of spiritual consolation is especially necessary when God is speaking to a person and urging decisions through interior affective experiences, but this discernment requires much reflection. The consolation of one's history is significant for decision-making because it carries a sense of wholeness, continuity and openness, qualities which are useful for judging the state of consolation needed for correct decisions.

The spiritual consolation of one's history can accompany the four phases. Thus, in the phase of remembering one's history the spiritual insight that God "is always faithful to his promises" can be experienced. In the phase of searching there is the consolation of spiritual understanding when a pattern is recognized. These two affective experiences, remembering and spiritual understanding, develop in the last two phases into the comprehensive consolation of one's history. In the phase of being whole, I experience my oneness with God in my total history, giving the sense of continuity, meaning, humility, and acceptance described in Chapter 7. Lastly, this consolation also contains an openness to the forward direction I perceive in my life relationship with God. As part of this openness, the affective experience of commitment to the forward direction discovered imparts the sense of freedom, desire, and obedience described in Chapter 8. Together, these affective elements make up the comprehensive consolation of one's history which helps in making correct decisions.

My own experience of guiding many people through the Spiritual Exercises of St. Ignatius Loyola taught me the value of appropriation and its accompanying consolation for correct decisions. But, because there are a number of decision-making processes and stages in the prayer experience of the Exercises, it was important to unravel them before applying appropriation. In doing this I have found that there are two kinds of knowledge coming from one's history, which are applicable in making decisions and also that these are related to two methods of making decisions found in the Exercises, the simple and sophisticated methods.

The two kinds of knowledge of one's personal history are: (1) the reflective knowledge of one's past history coming from much consideration of the events of one's total life; (2) the affective knowledge that comes from appropriating one's history in faith and results in the spiritual consolation of that history. The first kind is a knowledge predominantly achieved through the phases of remembering all of one's life and searching for the pattern in it. The second kind is the experience described in the phases of being whole and of being open to the forward direction discovered.

I do not want to leave the impression that there is no affective element in the knowledge gained in the phases of remembering and of searching for the pattern in one's life or that reflective knowledge is not present and significant in the phases of being whole and of being open. Nor do I wish to suggest that experiences of consolation are not important for the simple method of making decisions or that reasoning and reflection are not needed in making decisions by the sophisticated method. My concern is to present the predominant elements of the first two phases and show how they differ from the predominant elements of the last two phases, and to show how the predominant elements of the last two phases especially serve the sophisticated method of making decisions.

Simple and Sophisticated Methods

In speaking of a simple method in contrast to a sophisticated method of decision-making, one has to be careful lest the impression is given that the simple is not as important as the sophisticated, or that the sophisticated method is so complicated as to detract from the truth and simplicity one looks for in the spiritual life.

The simple method tends to be more logical, flowing as it does from the value system presented by the Ten Commandments, the Church's Precepts, and the gospel message of charity. With an informed conscience we know right from wrong in a general way and we can apply this to a concrete situation. Even our historical experience of guilt and fulfillment, of reward and punishment is helpful. We desire to respond to the love of God revealed to us by the death of Jesus; we make this response by acts of love both for God and for our neighbor (*cf.* Mt. 25:31-46). With the help of these teachings of the Church, we can make proper Christian decisions in a simple straightforward way.

The sophisticated method becomes necessary when we have gained an awareness of God moving us to decisions through the interior experiences of spiritual consolation or desolation. Then we see that the more subtle spiritual forces of life are influencing our decisions for good or evil. We realize we must become more aware of the good and evil influences in the interior of our being and learn how to judge these in decisions and actions. At this point we find we need a more sophisticated process to help sort out our interior movements. We need to know true spiritual consolation and to recognize when we have experienced a true sense of union with God. We need to know the significance of such spiritual consolation in decision-making.

Simple Method of Making Decisions

The prolonged prayer experience designed by St. Ignatius includes "every way of preparing and disposing the soul to rid itself of all inordinate attachments, and, after their removal, of seeking and finding the will of God in the disposition of our life for the salvation of our soul" [1]. Some of these ways involve processes of decision-making that are relatively simple, and they have value in various circumstances: (1) when I am deciding and acting against my sinfulness, my selfish tendencies, and gross temptation; (2) when I am ridding myself of selfish interests; (3) when I am easily moved to decision; and (4) when I am deciding between two good alternatives.

(1) In reflecting upon one's spiritual state there is a simple method for dealing with sin and temptation. It is basically the practice of becoming aware of sin and defects, then of being sorry, and of making a resolution to amend. In this activity I seek to correct or improve myself. I can do this by praying over the commandments, the seven capital vices, or my use of the five senses. For example, I ask God our Lord for the grace to recognize my failures in the observance of the commandment, "Thou shalt not bear false witness against thy neighbor", and I discover where and how I tend to do this. Then I resolve to avoid such situations and pray to be truthful in the future. If I wish to deal with temptations, an elementary knowledge of how I am tempted in a gross way is helpful so that I can recognize the experience and avoid the results. With such temptations "the enemy is ordinarily accustomed to propose apparent pleasures. He fills their imagination with sensual delights and gratifications, the more readily to keep them in their vices and increase the number of their sins" [314].

(2) The process of overcoming selfish interests is at once simple and difficult. It can be a preparation for our other decisions or a part of a renewal of our life: "For every one must keep in mind that in all that concerns the spiritual life his progress will be in proportion to his surrender of self-love and of his own will and interests" [189]. When we reflect on our history and become aware of some selfish interest inhibiting our freedom, then in our desire to rid ourselves of the inhibition, this method is useful: we can beg our Lord to take away the object of our interest that we treasure so much: "We should insist that we desire it, beg for it, plead for it, provided, of course, that it be for the service and praise of the Divine Goodness" [157].

(3) Throughout a retreat, we are asked by St. Ignatius to follow certain instructions concerning our prayer. From the moment of awakening until going to sleep, we are asked to be attentive to the presence of God while waking, washing, eating, etc., as well as before each prayer period. The daily reflec-

tion on one's spiritual state is a further time to consider choices already made and those still in the offing. We begin each period of prayer with a decision in grace that all our "intentions, actions, and operations may be directed purely to the praise and service of His Divine Majesty" [46]. All these decisions are made by the simple method of responding to the commitment I have made to pray in this way.

Even very important decisions can be made simply. During such a prayer experience our wish to make a correct and good choice of a way of life simplifies itself. For God may so move and attract us that without hesitation, or the possibility of hesitation, we follow what is presented.

(4) At another time when our being is tranquil, that is, a time when we are not agitated by different interior movements and have a free and peaceful use of our reasoning process, we can use the simple method of deciding between two good alternatives. A relatively simple method is to weigh the advantages and disadvantages of the options and choose according to the reasons that appear more important.

The method is simple, but the state of freedom I need to make such a decision is difficult to attain: "I must be indifferent, without any inordinate attachment . . . I should be like a balance at equilibrium, without leaning to either side, that I might be ready to follow whatever I perceive is more for the glory and praise of God our Lord and for the salvation of my soul" [179]. Moreover, diligence and insight in prayer is required so that my choice may be worthy of God's confirmation (*cf.* [183]). The confirmation may be known by a continuing state of tranquility and the absence of negative experiences. On the other hand, an experience of such movement of spirits may indicate that I need to make use of a more sophisticated method of choice.

Appropriation and the Simple Method

While there is a sense of the historical in a prolonged prayer experience such as the Exercises, it is not of the same order as the appropriation of one's history described in this book. Still, the places in the prayer experience where one encounters the historical can become take-off points for a deeper entry into one's history. This can be seen in the instruction to reflect over one's prayer and give careful attention to preparation and recollection before each prayer period (*cf.* [77]). Also the director is instructed to help by questioning the retreatant about attitudes and the observance of details remotely and immediately concerned with prayer. "He will demand an account in detail of each one of these points" [6]. The historical can be seen in the meditation on one's sins where the first consideration is to make a record of one's sins: "I will call to mind all the sins of my life, reviewing year by year, and period by period" [56]. Similarly, to counter the enemy a complete knowledge is needed of one's weaknesses gained by historical consideration for, "Where he finds the defenses of external salvation weakest and most deficient, there he attacks and tries to take us by storm" [327]. Also, there is often a suggestion to examine or to check one's "growth" and "progress" in perfection. Still, in these instructions the historical is not considered with the fullness that I am suggesting.

When the appropriation of my whole history is brought to bear in a prayer experience such as the Exercises, the impact on the simple method is to give a larger sampling of reflective data. The phases of remembering and of searching for my life pattern give me many examples with which to compare the present decision. The appropriation of my history assists me by providing material for comparison. It may also encourage me to make a decision or confirm a decision once made. Knowing how God has treated me in the past can help in the many decision-making processes: striving against sins and defects, ridding myself of selfish interests, making good choices. Searching through my past experience of God, when considering my sin-history, can move me more quickly through fear of punishment to gratitude and sorrow. My history helps me to face the question about what I ought to do about selfish interests. I can learn from my very sinfulness how to prevent sinning with the help of God's grace. On the other hand, searching my history can indicate to me that I have overcome selfish interests. I discover that I have made some good choices in the past, with God's grace, which were truly fulfilling experiences. This remembering can move me to desire freedom and to make the better choice for God.

In the phases of remembering and searching for the patterns in my history I move through the steps of knowledge, desire and choice. Through reflection, I know my full historical life span, and this is different from the daily reflection of my spiritual state which is more particularized and concerns incidents of sins and virtues. These phases of appropriation are also helpful in motivating my desires because they take place within the overall dialogue with God. I am aware both of God's patient mercy over my lifetime and the encouraging power of grace towards my sins and disorder. This motivates me in sorrow and hope to correct or improve myself and to rid myself of selfish interests. Furthermore, the memory of how God has sustained me over my life and the discernment of the pattern of how he has drawn good out of evil and used me to help others stirs up within me the generosity and desire to make decisions that may entail suffering.

The Sophisticated Method of Making Decisions

The sophisticated method accepts the fact that our affective states (the inordinate, such as greed, envy, anger, lust, pride, and the ordered, such as love for God and neighbor), are very influential in our decision-making. This method, therefore, involves the recognition of interior affective movements and of true spiritual consolation as criteria for decision and action. The faith-appropriation of our history will assist us in this more sophisticated method because it not only confirms and encourages us to make proper Christian decisions but it gives us the consolation of our history which becomes a means of judging the true consolation needed for correct decisions.

When we wish to act responsibly in today's world, we are confronted with a great number of options. We may truly wish to fulfill the challenge of Vatican II to build a better world. "Hence it is clear that men are not deterred by the Christian message from building up the world, or impelled to neglect the welfare of their fellows. They are, rather, more stringently bound to do these very things" (*Vatican II* #34, pg. 233). Yet we are conscious of false motives and false ideologies. Authentic Christian decision-making has become more sophisticated. We have some awareness of what not to do concretely from the Commandments and other instructions of the Church. What to do positively is another question. We realize it is important but difficult for us to discover the interior urgings of God and his direction. We need a more sophisticated method for reaching positive decisions.

St. Ignatius outlines such a method in a series of instructions for choosing a way of life and for the distribution of alms. After placing oneself in a faith context with God and petitioning to know and follow the lead of his grace, there are four basic steps: (1) seeking the freedom to listen to God's word coming through the affective experiences of consolation and desolation; (2) considering the possibilities in freedom; (3) making a choice during the time of the affective state of true spiritual consolation; and (4) discovering the choice and its confirmation in such a consolation.

(1) This method is dependent on my own freedom to be open and to respond to whatever God reveals to me by means of the interior experiences of consolation and desolation. I am to listen and tend towards his word with desire to follow it. The freedom and desire flow from the awareness of God's love for me usually gained by remembering and reflecting on my history and from a conviction of the power of Christ's triumph over suffering and death in his resurrection experienced as conversion. Again, I seek the freedom, described earlier, to "be indifferent, without any inordinate attachment, so that I am not more inclined or disposed to accept the object in question than to relinquish it, nor to give it up than to accept it. I should be like a balance at equilibrium, without leaning to either side, that I might be ready to follow whatever I perceive is more for the glory of God our Lord and the salvation of my soul" [179]. Normally this freedom and desire is the result of long prayer and spiritual direction. (I have discussed how a person can gain this kind of freedom in my book, *Spiritual Freedom* (Guelph, 1972).

(2) When I wish to make decisions in the Lord I consider the possibilities in freedom. "Freedom" means that I am not inordinately confined by prior commitments or law and that I hold myself open to following whichever choice I experience as coming from God. Thus, in the choice of a way of life, or giving donations, or choosing an apostolate in terms of faith and justice, I consider each state of life in openness or in desire to give gifts to those most in need, or I allow my deepest desires to surface so that they may be an instrument of God's concern for the poor and oppressed. As I face these decisions I need to feel free from any prejudice about one way of life over another or from the inclination to give gifts to my relatives and friends or from the constraints of my comfortable life.

(3) In addition to this spiritual freedom, which is itself a consolation, the more sophisticated method relies on the affective experiencing and judging of true spiritual consolation. It is a time, "When much light and understanding are derived through experiences of desolation and consolation and discernment of diverse spirits" [176].

To know if this is the correct time for making authentic Christian decisions, we need to recognize the experience of spiritual consolation. This is gained by comparing previous affective experiences of true consolation with present experience. For when I am in true consolation a good influence guides and counsels me (*cf.* [318]).

(4) Similarly, during and at the end of a process we look for true consolation as a sign that God accepts and confirms our decision (*cf.* [183]). To judge if this affective experience is in harmony with true consolation a correct understanding of spiritual consolation is needed. The following description of St. Ignatius ought to be studied and appreciated.

I call it consolation when an interior movement is aroused in the soul, by which it is inflamed with love of its Creator and Lord, and as a consequence, can love no creature on the face of the earth for its own sake, but only in the Creator of them all. It is likewise consolation when one sheds tears that move to the love of God, whether it be because of sorrow for sins, or because of the sufferings of Christ our Lord, or for any other reason that is immediately directed to the praise and service of God. Finally, I call consolation every increase of faith, hope, and love, and all interior joy that invites and attracts to what is heavenly and to the salvation of one's soul by filling it with peace and quiet in its Creator and Lord. [*316*].

In using this sophisticated method I can most surely discover the best choice and its confirmation if I experience the spiritual consolation of union in mind and heart with Jesus Christ. In a prolonged prayer experience such as Ignatius' Exercises this begins with a period of purification. By the end of this period, I have gained some knowledge of the horrifying and destructive aspects of sin, and through grace I have realized the great personal love that Jesus has for me, dying as he does on the cross for my sins. After this purification I am able to focus more fully upon Jesus and to seek the consolation of "intimate knowledge of our Lord, who has become man for me, that I may love Him more and follow Him more closely" [104].

According to Ignatius, this love is engendered while I contemplate the mysteries of Christ's life and make the following petition first to Our Lady, then to our Lord, and finally to the Father after each prayer period.

. . . The grace to be received under His standard, first in the highest spiritual poverty, and should the Divine Majesty be pleased thereby, and deign to choose and accept me, even in actual poverty; secondly, in bearing insults and wrongs, thereby to imitate Him better, provided only I can suffer these without sin on the part of another, and without offense of the Divine Majesty [*147*].

I may even be led to seek the following attitude of affective relationship with Christ:

If we suppose the first and second kind attained, then whenever the praise and glory of the Divine Majesty would be equally served, in order to imitate and be in reality more like Christ our Lord, I desire and choose poverty with Christ poor rather than riches; insults with Christ loaded with them, rather than honors; I desire to be accounted as worthless and a fool for Christ, rather than to be esteemed as wise and prudent in this world. So Christ was treated before me. [*167*].

At such a time my being could be most in harmony with Christ's. This close attunement to Christ helps me to recognize when a decision is made in true consolation. I can be attentive to the spiritual movements affecting me as I focus on Jesus and his approach to life. For the love that moves and causes me to choose must descend from above, that is, from the love of God, so that before I choose I should perceive that the greater or less attachment for the object of my choice is determined by my love of the Lord (*cf.* [184, 237, 338]). At this time I may hope to judge more clearly whether or not my interior spiritual movements are in harmony with the mind and heart of Jesus, because I have gained much affective knowledge of him through the contemplations of the mysteries of his life.

The sophisticated elements in the four steps of this method are present in the recognizing of the time of spiritual consolation and in judging the significance of my interior spiritual movements as a decision is being considered. These elements are dependent on my affective union with Christ coming through prayer and comparing this consolation of union with my interior spiritual movements. The activity of appropriating heightens my awareness of consolation and its significance.

Appropriation and the Sophisticated Method

I have been emphasizing that the recognition of true spiritual consolation is of prime importance in the sophisticated method of making decisions. The appropriation of one's history assists the sophisticated method in such recognition because it gives me a comprehensive experience of spiritual consolation coming through my total life story as it is known in union with the mysteries of Christ's life. This comprehensive consolation may then become the main affective experience I use to judge the present consolation. In fact, when the present consolation is correct, I experience it as continuous and in harmony with the comprehensive consolation of my total history.

Because the presence of true spiritual consolation is discovered in the various interior movements, this appropriation is a further aid to the sophisticated method. This activity gives me an extensive knowledge of my interior spiritual movements. It brings to me an extensive knowledge of these movements as I have experienced them throughout my total life.

In a prayer experience such as the Exercises an awareness of the spiritual movements within me is attained by studying my thought processes as they develop over a short period of time. In this study I gain the art of recognizing the interior movements in my being and later applying this knowledge in making decisions.

The following advice is given by St. Ignatius to help us gain some knowledge of the interior movements in my being.

We must carefully observe the whole course of our thoughts. If the beginning and middle and end of the course of thoughts are wholly good and directed to what is entirely right, it is a sign that they are from the good angel. But the course of thoughts suggested to us may terminate in something evil, or distracting, or less good than the soul had formerly proposed to do. Again, it may end in what weakens the soul, or disquiets it; or by destroying the peace, tranquility, and quiet which it had before, it may cause disturbance to the soul. These things are a clear sign that the thoughts are proceeding from the evil spirit, the enemy of our progress and eternal salvation.

When the enemy of our human nature has been detected and recognized by the trail of evil marking his course and by the wicked end to which he leads us, it will be profitable for one who has been tempted to review immediately the whole course of the temptation. Let him consider the series of good thoughts, how they arose, how the evil one gradually attempted to make him step down from the state of spiritual delight and joy in which he was, till finally he drew him to his wicked designs. The purpose of this review is that once such an experience has been understood and carefully observed, we may guard ourselves for the future against the customary deceits of the enemy [*333-334*].

This advice about the origin of my thoughts is especially important when those thoughts are leading me to choices. It can help me in the sophisticated method when I am trying to discover if God, myself, or some other spirit is promoting a particular choice.

As I grow in awareness of the various interior movements, I realize that I can experience different attitudes of mind and heart with respect to the same physical or emotional state or action to be taken. For example, when I become sick, I may react in anger at the inconvenience or in relief that I don't have to work for awhile. Or again I may feel that this sickness is a punishment for sins or an opportunity to suffer for Christ's body. Similarly when experiencing anger or loneliness, I may in one way turn in on myself and be filled with self-pity and separated from God, but in another way I may feel led to think of Jesus in the Garden of Gethsemane and be moved to unite myself with his suffering. When I am deciding to carry out an action, I may experience fears or hopes before deciding, being loved or alone while deciding, doubts or trust in Christ's presence and strength when acting.

In the sophisticated method I do not determine whether the impetus of a decision is from God by looking at the object of choice, but rather by investigating my affective state spiritually when the object is suggested. The affective direction and intentionality in which my thoughts arise are the important discernment, as well as the affective position at the end of the process of my thoughts. I need to examine the process of thoughts to discover if they have a good source or an evil one: "If a cause precedes, both the good angel and the evil spirit can give consolation to a soul, but for a quite different purpose" [331]. Do I experience an affective movement towards or away from Christ and his life style? If it is towards Christ, I can judge that the consolation is true and from a good source. If it is away from Christ, I judge that the movement arises from an evil source. The judging of these thought processes arising from affective states is a practice that must be learned in order to make decisions in the sophisticated method.

The activity of appropriating my history in faith can give me this skill. As I gain the ability to remember, search, feel whole, and feel open with Christ, there arises a knowledge by connaturality. This means that I can have a type of sympathetic response to situations akin to that of Jesus. There is a remembering and searching with his Spirit and an experience of being whole and of being open in his Spirit.

The significance of the appropriation of one's history as I have described it for the sophisticated method is that, as an experience of spiritual consolation, it becomes a basis for judging incidental spiritual consolation. While consolation is the time for correct decisions (*cf.* [318]), the recognition of true spiritual consolation when seeking to do what is more for God's praise and glory requires much knowledge. Consoling feelings and desires often mask a false movement towards decision. The extensive knowledge of the interior movements that have occurred over one's total life can unmask the false movement. But, in addition, one needs the authenticity of the consolation of one's history as a check on the affective origin of the thought process.

Within the affective knowledge of my life and the comprehensive consolation of my history, the activity and affective experiences of the four phases give the kind of deep-felt knowledge that is necessary in judging the state of my being in terms of God's love moving me to decide. The phase of remembering evokes the affective experiences of my life as they have proven authentic by giving rise to good decisions in the past. Certain self-authenticating peak experiences add weight to the other affective experiences recalled. The phase of searching for pattern gives me an overall affective knowledge of the relationship between affective experiences and good decisions. The phase of being whole gives me the sense of rightness of an affective experience because it is in harmony with the wholeness of my life. The phase of openness gives the sense of forward direction in my life and thus an affective means of judging if the present decision is in line with this direction.

In terms of the four steps of the sophisticated method of making decisions, the four phases are very helpful. (1) When I am seeking freedom to listen to God's word coming through the affective experiences of consolation and desolation, the phase of remembering how God has been present throughout my life fills me with trust and hope as I face possible choices. The affective experience of having been remembered, with its accompanying trust and hope, leads me to the freedom I seek. (2) As I consider the possibilities available in such free choices, the phase of searching for pattern gives me a rundown of the many choices that have already been presented to me and a truly free knowledge of my capabilities in the Lord. (3-4) The last two steps of the sophisticated method rely on the knowledge of spiritual consolation for recognizing the time of correct decisions and its significance for choices and confirmation. For these reasons the phases of being whole and of being open are especially helpful for they are more directly concerned with the comprehensive affective experience accompanying appropriation.

In considering the activity of making authentic Christian decisions in today's world, the appropriation of one's history in faith is essential because our dialogue with God is a growing affair. The relationship between the will of God and mankind's place in the universe is not static but living. "Seeking and finding the will of God" should not be conceived to mean that God's will is something objectively set to be discovered. The expression refers rather to the free spirit of humanity moving forward and accepting the responsibility of making a better world in cooperation with God's love and urgings. In other words, the historical is to be found in the very growth of Christ's kingdom: the knowledge, love and following of Christ which builds this better world develops through the growing affective experience of spiritual consolation that is one's history.

Following the message in Deuteronomy, "The Word is very near you, it is in your mouth and in your heart" (Dt. 30:14), we can expect to find the answer to decision-making processes within ourselves. As we seek to know how to respond to the urgings and motions of God in our inner spirit, we will find the answers in our deepest desires as his adopted children intent on faith and justice, on kindness and compassion, on dying for the sake of the brethren (*cf.* Rm. 8:14-17; Ph.

2:13). These urgings have already been operative throughout our history. We but need to get in touch with them through the four phases of remembering, search, wholeness and openness and apply this interior knowledge to the methods of making decisions presented here.

Emergence

The appropriation of one's unique history in faith and the resulting consolation of that history take place differently in different persons; there are several signs that such an appropriation of my unique history in faith is emerging. An "approach" to my history in faith may precede the activity of appropriating it in faith. Thus I may begin to examine the history of my life to appreciate it. Convinced of its value, I may develop a faith-approach to my own history. Still, appropriation may not be emerging. This may be simply a time for gathering historical data. Then the elements of my life can start to become the matter of my prayer in a meditative sense.

I may get many insights about myself and my actions from the historical data. Some may lead to comfort and joy in remembering, some to sorrow, some to anger, some to the need for forgiveness or for compassion towards others. If I move to contemplate my life in terms of God's constant presence, certain signs may begin to emerge that are properly part of the appropriation of my unique history in faith. These are more than the gathering of data which is part of a faith-approach to my whole life. What are these signs? There are three in particular which indicate that this activity and its accompanying consolation is emerging: freedom, responsibility, and development. They may come at any time or through any form of prayer.

When I pray over the significance of Jesus' death and resurrection a new sense of hope in myself begins to emerge and it expresses a different freedom in relationship to God. This freedom comes from a sense of value of myself as an object of God's love and even more, as an instrument of God's love for others. It is accompanied by an experience of true humility.

A second sign of appropriation is a sense of responsibility towards myself and everyone else. I gain a certain objectivity towards myself and others as human beings. I am not only able to forgive others who have offended me, but I am now open to experiencing the forgiveness of God by forgiving myself and having compassion upon myself. This new sense of responsibility expresses itself in a willingness to go beyond myself when moved by God to do so.

The third sign is an awareness of myself developing as part of a positive outlook on my history. This last may naturally move me to an initial experience of the consolation of my history. These three signs can occur in any order and often will be intertwined. Their emergence will usually be quickened if I am in the midst of a serious decision.

How does one describe the first sign, this new sense of freedom? It is different from the freedom called indifference or detachment in classical spiritual literature. In classical terminology "indifference" and "detachment" refer to the stance I adopt toward other persons and things as I attempt to discover my concrete relationship with God here and now. The freedom we are speaking about is different in kind and probably in degree, and it has to do mainly with the way I feel God relates to me, rather than how I can use things in my service of him. Thus, as a result of meditating on his forgiving love and on Jesus' death on the cross for my sins, I become aware that God is constant in his love for me. He is always there to forgive me openly and freely, with compassion and kindness, not grudgingly (*cf.* Rm. 5:6-11, Lk. 6:27-38). With this awareness there emerges the spiritual insight that I don't have to please God to gain his love. It is the experience that God's love is not constraining me but freeing me. It is a love that is encouraging me rather than coercing me. It is a love that allows me to err and sin, a love that seeks to save rather than to condemn (*cf.* Jn. 3:17 and 12:47). From then on I know that my fear of God is coming not from him but from myself or from the social context of my life. My experience of freedom seems to agree with John's first letter: "In love there can be no fear, but fear is driven out by perfect love: because to fear is to expect punishment, and anyone who is afraid is still imperfect in love" (1 Jn. 4:18).

The second sign occurs as I realize that I am being called to respond as an adult in my dialogue with God. I am not called to respond as a child hoping for reward or fearing punishment or seeking total protection. This new sense of responsibility is the opposite of resignation or fatalism for it acknowledges that the free adult has a part to play in the building of God's kingdom. In my desire to be an adult, a deeper appreciation of myself as a "contemplative in action" arises; my own history becomes a source of revelation of the mystery of God within me. This awareness does not diminish my awareness that I am a child of God. But I realize now that I am a child of the Father in the same manner as my brother Jesus whose responsibility towards the world meant that he gave his life. St. Paul speaks about such coming of age in reference to the law. His words are applicable here: "The law was to be our guardian until the Christ came and we could be justified by faith. Now that that time has come we are no longer under that guardian, and you are, all of you, sons of God through faith in Christ Jesus" (Ga. 3:24-26).

The new awareness of freedom and responsibility go hand in hand. It is difficult to determine which precedes and which follows. This experience is an awesome one and may tend to paralyze me at first. Eventually, with support and encouragement it is seen and accepted as a more mature living of my life with God. In faith I accept my immediate responsibility for the world without going into panic. I know I am limited in talent, holiness and scope. I turn to God in prayer for light and strength.

New consciousness of freedom and responsibility now gives rise to the third sign. I become aware that I have been developing spiritually, as well as physically and psychologically. There is growth in my personal relationship with the Trinity. I know about my natural history, physical and psychological; I discover that I have a spiritual history as well and that these histories are related. My history, I know, is important. My own development as well as that of all the human race and of the Church, is part of the free, mature relationship with God. Again, I come to this awareness in a spirit of hope for my future actions and not with a crippling fear.

The awareness of sinfulness, limitation, weakness, growth and development in all persons and in myself is accepted in a new way. These are not seen only as imperfections to be overcome, but as part of my being that I am to work with. I become conscious in faith that God supports me as one who develops, not only physically and psychologically but also spiritually. There is not some perfect me, totally formed, against which I measure myself as I sin or perform virtuous acts. God's act of creating me is not like a static sculpture that my sins gradually deform. Rather, I have a sense of myself as dynamic and I know the dynamic relationship with God is good. When Genesis says, "God saw all he made, and indeed it was very good" (Gn. 1:31), our freedom and our responsibility was the peak of his creation.

The human race develops in its relationship with God. The Church develops in her life with God. I develop in my life with God and this development is dependent on the other two. In this dynamic sense I realize that my faith is given to me historically and grows with my history. It is part of my history.

Contemplation

At any moment the heightening awareness of myself as historical may be the occasion for emergence of appropriation. It might come during meditative prayer on my history. It could happen when I am reflecting on some of the various attributes of God: his providential care, his love-relationship with Israel as father, mother, husband, his desire to give and forgive, his role as savior. At another time, the consideration of my sin in the context of times, places, and persons could bring an awareness of a continuous history that is grace-filled with forgiveness. Or I may begin to see my own history in faith as I reflect on the history of Jesus Christ. The continuity of my history at any time during the thirty-day Exercises may prove to be the occasion for this appropriation in faith.

Contemplating the mysteries of Christ's life is a type of

prayer that seems propitious to this emergence. Such contemplation is a special form of mental prayer. It is different from meditation, from prayers of personal investigation, from the simple prayer of quiet or presence. It is a form of prayer in which I accept in faith that Jesus Christ is risen and is Lord of history. I accept that the earthly life of Jesus is important for me. I accept that Jesus can put me in contact with his earthly life and that the gospels are the medium for this kind of prayer. Yet, such prayer includes the present and takes into account my own historical context while praying. The way this is usually expressed is that I discover the mystery of my own being by coming into contact with the mystery of Jesus Christ who lived and died but rose from the dead.

Contemplation, then, allows Jesus to reveal himself to me in a less ecstatic and more free way than the immediate experience of the Godhead would allow (Think of Paul's experience on the way to Damascus in Acts 9:1-9). The whole of myself is present with the whole of Christ as I come in contact with the person of Jesus. This means all of my historical background is present and so is Jesus. The development of humanity along with the development of the Church down the centuries is present to me in contemplation (*cf. Vatican II*, pgs. 245-6).

Because Jesus experienced historically the friendship and final approval of God, the Father, I too may expect to find friendship and approval of God in my own history. My belief in the resurrection is the beginning of this contemplative form of prayer. This same belief serves as a basis for appropriating my history in faith.

In contemplating I experience the desires, hopes, fears, sufferings, challenges, and prayers of Jesus; and I experience my own desires, hopes, etc. This is because my own unique historical experiences are united with Jesus' through the Spirit that is given (*cf.* Rm. 8:14-29; Ga. 2:20; Col. 1:24). One result of this method of prayer is to enable me to be with Jesus from his incarnation to his resurrection. One remembers the concern of Peter that Judas be replaced in the apostolic college by one who had been with them "right from the time when John was baptizing until the day when he was taken up from us—and he can act with us as a witness to his resurrection" (Ac. 1:22).

St. Ignatius Loyola gives a fairly simple but traditional method of doing this kind of contemplation (*cf.* [101-117]). The grace I seek in these contemplations indicates that much more than an exercise in the imagination is to take place since I ask for a personal knowledge of Jesus in order to love and be with him. When I am contemplating I may become aware that some mysteries of Christ's life such as the incarnation have a more transcendental quality and that some such as the nativity have a more historical quality.

This may mean that I experience less reflection on myself in a contemplation on the incarnation than on the nativity. But when my reflection shifts from what I see and hear in the mystery to myself I have entered more completely into contemplation. I become part of the mystery that I am contemplating (*cf.* [114-116, 194]). Jesus is the focal point of my contemplation, but I am also present with him. Now this very type of contemplating can prepare me to appropriate my history in faith because I become intimately involved with the very history of Jesus Christ, the lord of history.

Jesus' continual need to contemplate suggests that he also is part of the free universe that God created to develop dynamically. His praying indicates a dependency on the Father and a spiritual development in himself. My contemplating puts me in touch with the paradigm of such development which, in turn, is so necessary for my own growth.

Along with these three signs, a new experience of consolation can come. I experience a new sense of personal value as a developing person and face the option of suffering with Christ in a new way. There is also an awareness that my work down the years has been important for building God's kingdom and that it will be important in the future. St. Ignatius makes reference to this in a letter to Teresa Rejadella when describing desolation: ". . . our old enemy now puts before us all possible difficulties to turn us aside from what we have begun. . . . he suggests that we are entirely forgotten by God our Lord, and we come to imagine that we are separated from Our Lord in everything and that however much we have done and however much we want to do, it is of no value whatever. Thus he strives to bring us into distrust of everything . . ." (Rahner, Hugo, S.J.: *Saint Ignatius Loyola Letters to Women*, Herder and Herder, New York, 1960, p. 334).

With this new faith awareness of the importance of my unique history there comes the consolation expressed in the desire to serve the Lord: "I can do all things in Christ who strengthens me" (*cf.* Ph. 4:13).

The Director's Role During Emergence

A consideration of the overall responsibility of spiritual directors can help me understand their position when appropriation in faith is emerging or growing. Generally speaking, the role of spiritual directors is threefold. They are to help me be open to God's initiatives in my life and so to be ready to follow the inspirations of the Trinity. This requires spiritual freedom. Directors are also to help me recognize the activity of God so that I can follow the Trinity's inspirations and reject others. This means discernment. Directors are also present to encourage me to respond to those inspirations when they are recognized as coming from the Trinity. This is the move to commitment. So directors are to assist me in the activities of freedom, discernment, and commitment. In appropriating my unique history these activities take on a new significance.

Prayer is the basic instrument for these activities. What happens between God and me is the platform for discussion, sharing and direction. The matter for prayer and the manner of prayer may vary. Whether the director suggests sacred scripture, the documents of the Church, current events, the *Spiritual Exercises*, or any other matter for prayer; whether meditation, *lectio divina*, contemplation, prayer of quiet, Christian yoga, or any other manner of prayer is suggested, the director is interested in the state of the retreatant's freedom, discernment, and commitment *vis-a-vis* God.

Freedom

My stance towards myself, other persons and other things, tells the director much about my spiritual freedom. Do I stand easy with life as a responsible developing Christian or does this make me anxious? The results of prayer can tell the director more than much discussion. In prayer, images of God are revealed, fears are brought to the surface, special yearnings are experienced as I consider my past history. Through articulation, discernment and support, the director helps me to correct false images of God and to meet my worst fears and temptations. These become the focal point for receiving freedom from God. The director can now introduce suitable material and be a support to me as I seek freedom from all other things but God. The director's own faith can encourage me to pray through my most fearful and repugnant expectations as these surface from my own concrete history.

Discernment

When spiritual freedom has been attained, the director judges that I am ready to make responsible decisions. Now the director's role is to help me discern what I am to do through consolations and desolations, while present to Christ in mystery. Of course, the director is dependent on the experience coming from my prayer and past history.

The director needs my articulation of these experiences for this discernment. Articulation of my past spiritual history can be of two kinds. One might be a short written biography of my spiritual history. This will be very helpful to my director as basic background from which he can ask further questions and receive a more affective articulation from me. However, my description of praying over my history is often more significant to my director than the written account of my spiritual history. Yet, the writing of such an account, as well as a spiritual journal may assist me to appreciate my spiritual history and so articulate it more accurately to my director.

The director's role as discerner tends to be more of an aid to me helping me compare present and past experiences for I am the final discerner of my own experience. Finally, the director lends support and faith by encouraging me to follow the lead of God in my life. This lead will agree with my deepest true desires and past experiences of God's initiatives. The director, therefore, helps me to get in touch with these deepest desires and their past fulfillment through experiences of prayer.

Commitment

The conviction of directors at this stage is important. They should realize that these three activities are important for the one directed, and believe that God can give spiritual freedom to this person, that God desires to give it, and that God gives it without destroying the person. They can hope that God's action in the one being directed is fulfilling and gives an experience of desire beyond the ordinary. Directors have to trust that the best course of action will be made known to the person and that God will give the grace of commitment for the decision being made.

In helping others appropriate their unique history in faith the spiritual director performs three functions similar to the above three of freedom, discernment, and commitment. The director helps prepare retreatants for the activity of appropriating their history in faith. The director is present to recognize if the retreatants are on the verge of appropriating their history in faith, properly speaking. The director encourages the retreatants to enter more completely into the activity of appropriating their history and then of using this appropriation in the discerning process.

Directors will be better equipped to help others in this activity if they have done it themselves. This means they will approach their own lives as mystery rather than as problem. Thus, the contemplative approach to one's history will be present. Directors may experience themselves as mystery in sensing their own creaturehood, or sinfulness, or vocation, or union, or historical development.

The director's own experience of appropriating helps in recognizing the position of retreatants. Are they asking questions about their history? Are they taking a faith-approach to their history? Are they gathering historical data? Have they moved to a new sense of freedom, responsibility, development, indicating the emergence of this appropriation of their own history in faith? Is there a sense of their unique history akin to that of creaturehood, sinfulness, companionship with Jesus. The director, sensing these things happening, may wait or encourage the one directed to enter more deeply into the activity of appropriation in faith.

The director's own experience while making decisions will help in the triple role of preparing others for an historical approach to their life, of recognizing the emergence of the activity of appropriation, and of encouraging this activity. Directors appreciate that temptation may come under the guise of light and of the historical element implied in these insights. So they will point this out to these persons at the appropriate time. As retreatants experience temptations under the guise of light a pattern will present itself. It is then that the director may begin to ask retreatants if this pattern fits into their historical experience. In this way the historical issue can emerge. This questioning is enough to have retreatants begin the process of appropriating their history in faith.

No doubt, pattern is better suited to the experience of temptation to evil, than to the Spirit's invitation to good. The temptations to evil come from finite sources and so a pattern can be discerned, whereas, the invitations to good are from the infinite possibilities in the Trinity, the source of love and goodness (*cf.* 1 Jn. 4:7-10). Yet with this awareness of pattern in the history of one's sinfulness and temptations to evil, there also emerges the awareness of one's personal history of redemption. The director can now encourage retreatants to investigate their own history of redemption and invitation to the good as well as the special experiences of going beyond themselves in compassion, patience, kindness and generosity.

Directors should always be aware they are meant to follow the lead of the Trinity when applying the spiritual insights from their own life to that of another. Also, without question, the validity of their own insights has to be judged against that of the Church and of the experience of her saints.

From their own experience directors may see that the preparation for and the emergence of their own historical appropriation in faith took place while contemplating the mysteries of the life of Jesus as given in the New Testament. While directors may wonder if they may set out intentionally to bring about this activity of appropriating one's history in another, they should be aware that in helping that person to contemplate the mysteries of Christ's life the activity of appropriating may emerge. A director might surmise that this kind of contemplation is appealing today for the reasons already given above (*cf. Vatican II* pgs. 206, 261). People are realizing in faith that the earthly life of Jesus depicted in the gospels is intimately related to their own life (*cf. Vatican II* pgs. 218, 220, 222). At the same time, they are conscious of themselves as developing historically (*cf. Vatican II*, pgs. 204, 240, 243-6) and are intrigued by the value of their free actions (*cf. Vatican II* pgs. 214, 232, 262-3). So, indirectly, we can say that helping persons learn to contemplate the mysteries of Christ's life is also a preparation for helping them to appropriate their own unique history in faith.

It may be that during a prolonged prayer experience of thirty days a director will see this activity emerging. But, then again, it may only emerge with the final prayer exercise, such as *The Contemplation* described in Chapter 4. In this case further direction and encouragement will have to take place after the retreat. This will become part of the process in ongoing direction.

THE ROLE OF THE SPIRITUAL DIRECTOR

These comments are intended to help a spiritual director come to more fully developed principles for guiding others during the time of decision-making.

A. Discerning the context in which decisions are made

The director helps the one being directed discover the context and method for making decisions. Is the context rather simple and straightforward or is it more sophisticated? If the context involves moving away from sins or enslaving attachments, the decisions involved may be straightforward. At other times the director helps the person become aware that a more sophisticated method of decision-making is needed and will have to instruct the one being directed in the use of the method.

B. Determining the presence of spiritual freedom with respect to the decision to be made

Gradually the person learns through direction to recognize when interior movements are leading towards Christ or towards self-centeredness. The one being directed is helped to see the harmonization or consistency of this movement with one's whole past history. The person is taught to be humble in consolation and how to handle oneself in times of desolation. When repugnances or blocks become evident the person can be taught to act against these repugnances by holding oneself "as if" free from them by praying earnestly to the Lord to be given the very thing feared, if it be the Lord's will (*cf.* [16, 157]). When the one being directed is in a state of sufficient spiritual freedom, the more precise elements of the method of decision making can be given. Is it a matter of a simple decision which emerges after spiritual freedom is attained? Would it be advisable to determine alternatives, weigh them, and judge according to the quality of the alternatives arrived at? Should the only method be the sophisticated method of recognizing true spiritual consolation and judging its significance?

C. Bringing the appropriation of one's history to bear on the decision

During the above process the director assists the person to see the significance of one's history as a decision is being made. The director encourages the phase of remembering so that the person may find light from similar past experiences of decision-making. Is the process similar to correct processes of the past? Are blindnesses or inordinate desires from the past recurring? As the person is weighing the decision the director encourages a searching through one's history to recall the pattern of God's initiatives once again. After a tentative decision is reached, the director suggests that the one being directed also recall the affective experiences of being whole and being open and place these alongside the present affective experience of consolation present in the tentative decision to see if they harmonize. This may require a return to contemplating one's life within the mysteries of the passion and resurrection of Jesus's life, since the affective experiences of being whole with one's history and being open to the forward direction in one's life find their paradigm in the passion, death, and resurrection of Jesus.

EXERCISE

Recognizing the consolation of my history when I am making decisions

Introduction

That is why I am continually recalling the same truths to you, even though you already know them and firmly hold them. I am sure it is my duty, as long as I am in this tent, to keep stirring you up with reminders, since I know the time for taking off this tent is coming soon, as our Lord Jesus Christ foretold to me. And I shall take great care that after my own departure you will still have a means to recall these things to memory.

It was not any cleverly invented myths that we were repeating when we brought you the knowledge of the power and the coming of our Lord Jesus Christ; we had seen his majesty for ourselves. He was honored and glorified by God the Father, when the Sublime Glory itself spoke to him and said, "This is my Son, the Beloved; he enjoys my favor." We heard this ourselves, spoken from heaven, when we were with him on the holy mountain. (2 Peter 1:12-18)

Here Peter is recalling the peak experience of Mount Tabor (Mt. 17:1-8) and also the movement of spirits in his own life. Out of these affective experiences he makes decisions on how to instruct the Christians.

Suggested Approaches

I ask the Lord for the grace to recognize the place of the

appropriation of my personal history in faith for correct decision making.

I will do this by asking the Lord to help me recall how an historical approach to my own life began.

I ask to recognize how a new sense of freedom, adult response and development began to take place in me.

I will recall the impact of contemplating the mysteries of Jesus' human life and my own for the activity of appropriating my own history in faith.

I will ask for the insight into the way this activity frees me from false images of God, fears and temptations.

I will ask to know how this activity of appropriating my history in faith enhances the gift of discernment, especially how the pattern of my history helps me to recognize deception under the guise of light.

I will ask the Lord for light and a sense of harmony as I make these comparisons:

I will compare my affective experience from the appropriation of my history in faith with the experiences of consolation in times of correct decision.

I will make a similar comparison with the experiences when I have been deceived; and when I have had peak religious experiences; and with the description given by St. Ignatius in the *Spiritual Exercises*:

In souls that are progressing to greater perfection, the action of the good angel is delicate, gentle, delightful. It may be compared to a drop of water penetrating a sponge.

The action of the evil spirit upon such souls is violent, noisy, and disturbing. It may be compared to a drop of water falling upon a stone.

In souls that are going from bad to worse, the action of the spirits mentioned above is just the reverse [*335*].

10 CONSOLATION AND COMMUNITY DECISIONS

Jesus was going up to Jerusalem, and on the way he took the Twelve to one side and said to them, 'Now we are going up to Jerusalem, and the Son of Man is about to be handed over to the chief priests and scribes. They will condemn him to death and will hand him over to the pagans to be mocked and scourged and crucified; and on the third day he will rise again.'

Then the mother of Zebedee's sons came with her sons to make a request of him, and bowed low; and he said to her, 'What is it you want?' She said to him, 'Promise that these two sons of mine may sit one at your right hand and the other at your left in your kingdom'. 'You do not know what you are asking' Jesus answered. 'Can you drink the cup that I am going to drink?' They replied, 'We can'. 'Very well,' he said 'you shall drink my cup, but as for seats at my right and my left, these are not mine to grant; they belong to those to whom they have been allotted by my Father.'

When the other ten heard this they were indignant with the two brothers. But Jesus called them to him and said, 'You know that among the pagans the rulers lord it over them, and their great men make their authority felt. This is not to happen among you. No; anyone who wants to be great among you must be your servant, and anyone who wants to be first among you must be your slave, just as the Son of Man came not to be served but to serve, and to give his life as a ransom for many. (Mt. 20:17-28)

Chapter 9 presented a method of decision-making that pointed to the appropriation of one's personal history in faith as a key element in the process. This method was explained in the context of individual concerns. The process involved prayer and insights gained during a prolonged prayer experience such as the Exercises of St. Ignatius Loyola. The context and method of prayer was to put one affectively in touch with Christ as he is presented in the scriptural mysteries of his life, reflecting all the time on the significance of one's own life story. The necessary elements of spiritual freedom and of judging the interior spiritual movements experienced in correct decisions was considered in terms of one's personal spiritual history.

While a person might do much consulting before the retreat and seek good spiritual counsel during it, the one praying is making the decision alone, albeit with and in the Lord. The appropriation in faith of one's personal history gives an affective state that is important for decisions in the private realm. A similar affective state of being is important for decisions in the public realm. This brings the person a further step in the making of decisions. It is the process of making decisions within a community.

Unilateral and Multilateral Decisions

All personal decisions are social. This means that they affect other persons directly or indirectly. Personal decisions can be experienced as made alone (in a private realm) or as made jointly with others (in a public realm). They can be considered as unilateral or multilateral decisions with private or public results.

The process for making decisions in a directed prayer experience is structured to help me take unilateral decisions and actions which concern me as an individual. The awareness of a call from God to a state of life and a fitting response is such a decision. I alone make this decision, and I am free to respond to this call or not without any inhibiting guilt feelings. Such decisions are unique, existential, and the result of my own judgment, even though I may seek much advice and seriously consider the social repercussions. A second example of such a decision is the conversion to the faith of a Christian community. A third example is that of two persons considering marriage. Here each person makes a unilateral decision with respect to the other. A further example is the proposal of a group of women or men to form a religious order. There is a written account of how Ignatius Loyola and his first companions established many safeguards so that such free decisions could be made by each person. These men did not wish to coerce one another, as they were trying to decide if they should form a religious order with the vow of obedience to one of their number.

There are also decisions persons make in conjunction with others which I would classify as multilateral decisions. These include the decisions a husband or wife makes within their marriage covenant or those a professed religious with the vows of poverty, chastity, and obedience makes within a religious order. In an extended sense, officials of government and the Church may also make such decisions as a consequence of their positions of authority or oaths of office. Such decisions flow from a publicly recognized bond of union with others and declare, in some way, the existence of this union, either to the other members of thc community or beyond it. The nature of the bond of union will determine the seriousness with which such decisions are made and considered by others. Social clubs and the like do not impart to decisions the same seriousness as do covenant communities with a true religious affiliation (Christian, Moslem, Jew, Hindu), or a family, or a religious order.

"Covenant" is a scriptural term describing a relationship between God and mankind. In the Old and New Testament it implies a blood relationship and a bond of union that is unbreakable. God is the guarantee of the permanence of the covenant because he is always faithful to his promises (Heb. 10:23). Jesus sets up such a covenant with all believers by the sacrifice of his life, "This cup is the new covenant in my blood which will be poured out for you" (Lk. 22:20). Within the covenant of Jesus and the Church (Eph. 5:29-32) there are approved covenanted groups such as marriages and religious orders.

After coming to a vocation decision and acting upon it by a unilateral decision, I may enter a covenant with other persons. Then my decisions that concern other persons enter the public realm because the bond of union includes all the other members in the covenant body. Christ expresses this most forcefully in the vocation to marriage when he declares, "They are no longer two, therefore, but one body" (Mt. 19:6). After such an entry into covenant, my decisions will be made communally. All my personal decisions now made are not only social but multilateral. By this I mean that there is a mutual effort not only in coming to decisions but in taking responsibility for them. This effort is present in the expressions of the decision and in carrying the decision into action, even if the mutuality is limited on the part of some to approval and encouragement.

My entrance into a covenant relationship means that I am no longer an individual person in my decision-making but a member of a covenant body. For this reason, the Church, married couples, religious orders, surround these covenants with safeguards in the form of oaths and vows. Religious orders devise methods in their constitutions by which decisions and actions within this covenant body are to be made and judged to harmonize or not with the urgings and consolation of God. Those in positions of spiritual government are bound by this aspect of the covenant when making public decisions.

I experience an aspect of multilateral decision on the receiving-end when I seek to enter a covenant group or to establish a new covenant group. The Church makes such a decision to accept persons entering her body by baptism, or to be distributors of sacraments as priests or to establish new covenant groups such as families by marriage or religious orders or other covenant institutes. While a group of men or women may come to a consensus of unilateral decisions that they should become a religious order and live under obedience, still this is dependent on the Church's multilateral decision for its implementation. In this, the Church's decision to establish this order is a confirmation of God's call in their unilateral decisions. Just as the father of the bride declares the decision of the bride's family in the public realm during the wedding ceremony, so too religious communities go through such a decision in judgment of a person's unilateral decision at three important moments: entry into the novitiate, vows, final vows.

Appropriating the Community's Unique History

When a man and a woman create a new covenant group by

their marriage vows and the approved decision of the Church, they enter into a new dynamic of decision-making. Because they are only two persons, it is possible that all decisions be made after much dialogue and communal discernment. In this effort the couple may realize the need to get in touch with each other's feelings and attitudes. This search may take them back into the unique personal history of each partner and the attempt to appropriate it in faith. But they also have a common experience of the life they have lived together as husband and wife. The effort also to appropriate this unique but communal history in faith can also be of great value in making decisions. They may learn that the criterion of good decisions in the Lord is the experience of love moving beyond the family, of a communal life which is related to all the mysteries of Christ's life and is in union with the larger covenant body of the Church. Reflecting on such experiences can give them an affective knowledge of the true spiritual consolation of their unique but communal history.

There is a similar but more complex dynamic when a person enters a covenant group of many adult members, such as a secular institute, a religious order, or a lay group such as a Christian Life Community. When I make my unilateral decision to join a covenant group, I move into a situation in which I will be involved with this group in multilateral decisions. So I am asked to study its constitutions and other writings. If I am going to be united to this group by such decisions in the public realm, I will have to move from the letter of the group's law, as found in the constitutions, common rules, or house rules, to its spirit. These laws and rules are good and necessary in much the same way as Paul says: "this new covenant, which is not a covenant of written letters but of the Spirit: the written letters bring death, but the Spirit gives life" (2 Co. 3:6).

The activity of appropriating the community's history is the method for attaining the community's spirit. I know the presence of this spirit by the spiritual consolation of the community's history. I truly need and should desire to be united in mind and heart with this group. Then I can be critical, argue, cajole, and present my deepest apostolic desires, as well as be sorry for the sins, shortcomings, and disappointments of the group in the Lord.

The head of such communities is Jesus Christ who left his Father to unite himself with the Church.

. . . a man never hates his own body, but he feeds it and looks after it; and that is the way Christ treats the Church, because it is his body—and we are its living parts. For this reason, a man must leave his father and mother and be joined to his wife, and the two will become one body. This mystery has many implications; but I am saying it applies to Christ and the Church (Eph. 5:29-32).

Within this body of the Church and at certain moments in history, a person or a group of persons is inspired to establish a religious order and to receive approval from the Church. These events and those that follow make up the history of the foundation. I believe that one can discover a subtle interplay between the experience and the spirit of the founders and the community's ongoing history.

If I wish to appropriate my order's history, I will attempt to unite myself with the experience of the founders, compare this with the order's history down the years and then compare these events in turn with my own personal history. As in the appropriation of my own unique history, I compare my own life to that of Christ, so here I do the same with that of the founders. While I cannot enter into contemplation of the founders' lives as I can with Christ's life, still I can consider how the history of the founders includes my own in its destiny. I am able to see the parallels in my own history and desires with those of the founders. Appropriating this knowledge in an affective way gives me the consolation of history within this covenant community.

There is also the appropriation of the history of the order as it grows down through the years. This is much like the history of a family. The very historical experience of the institute enters into the present state of the community that I am part of. I know these facts of history and accept them as part of my own spiritual ancestry. This history was created by my religious ancestors, both sinful and holy. The Spirit moves from where one has been to where one is now. God goes along with us and has done so with this spiritual ancestry of mine. The order's constitutions are enfleshed and personified in each succeeding generation. With such an identity and a history I can hope to interpret the spirit of the constitutions for today in keeping with the experience and the spirit of the founder. Hopefully, this openness will result in a dynamic development of the founders' spirit in me as I move into the future.

Many aspects of this history can be considered. Such factors as the time, numbers, geography, leaders, or apostolic work may evoke very little affective reaction. But other elements in this history may stir up much affective response.

For an apostolic order that is vitally concerned with faith and justice, the investigation into these aspects in the apostolic history are important. Where has the order's effort been successful in this regard? Why? Where has the effort of the order failed? Why? The judgments will be made in terms of Christian principles such as John gives:

This is the message as you heard it from the beginning: that we are to love one another; not to be like Cain, who belonged to the Evil One and cut his brother's throat; cut his brother's throat simply for this reason, that his own life was evil and his brother lived a good life. You must not be surprised, brothers, when the world hates you; we have passed out of death and into life, and of this we can be sure because we love our brothers. If you refuse to love, you must remain dead; to hate your brother is to be a murderer, and murderers, as you know, do not have eternal life in them. This has taught us love —that he gave his life for us; and we too, ought to give up our lives for our brothers. If a man who was rich enough in this world's goods saw that one of his brothers was in need, but closed his heart to him, how could the love of God be living in him? My children, our love is not to be just words or mere talk, but something real and active. (1 Jn. 3:11-18)

The interpretation of an order's history might also include the words of John the Baptist, "Christ must grow greater, I must grow smaller," (Jn. 3:30).

An affective approach to this history is important. Do I

identify affectively with the founders and later groups in the order's history? Do I experience sin, joy, suffering, failure, rejection, blessings, success, with them? Such prayerful reflection on these elements in the order's history is important for their appropriation in faith and the resulting consolation that aids me in decision-making.

Such activity is a present-day expression of being a contemplative in action. Most founders of religious orders realized that action is to flow out of contemplation over Christ's life and that reflection on action is to judge it. For the "love that moves and causes one to choose must descend from above" [184]. This activity of appropriating the order's ongoing apostolic history gives the affective experience (consolation) needed to judge a potential decision and judge an action as an expression of a "love that descends from above."

The four phases of memory, search, wholeness and openness to the community's history are present here. At each stage I compare my own unique history and integrate it with the history of the community. This activity and its consolation would seem to be part of the experience of knowing and appreciating the "grace of our vocation."

Spiritual Direction and Spiritual Government

In the multilateral process of decision-making in a religious order the individual member has two sources of assistance. These are spiritual direction and spiritual government. Spiritual direction is designed to help spiritual government, not to replace it. Spiritual government is the final aid for the person in making public decisions and actions with the community.

I will express my thoughts in terms of an active order, although much of what I say applies also to a contemplative order. What I say about a member can also refer to a group. What I say about a governor or superior can also be said about a governing body. The process of making a decision towards an apostolic work also applies to decisions about community life.

The role of a spiritual director is different from the role of a spiritual governor. It is good if a spiritual governor has had some experience in spiritual direction. But it is more important that the governor encourage members to seek out spiritual direction regarding a decision. This kind of direction concerning a decision is quite different from the support type of direction where the director is basically helping the person communicate with Christ in prayer. The support type of spiritual direction is more enlightening about the presence of interior spiritual movements. The spiritual direction in a time of serious decision concerns itself with the use and significance of these movements for making authentic Christian decisions. I would like to discuss the way in which the two persons, that is, the spiritual director and the spiritual governor, help another member of the community to make these personal, yet public decisions.

Through the covenant bond with the Church, the spiritual governor has been given authority to interpret the law of the religious order in particular instances and to send members on assignments. This means the governor has the "grace of office" in such actions with reference both to the life style of a community and to its apostolate. Today, we realize that these rights of interpreting and sending on mission require discernment of spirits by the spiritual governor and that this discernment should take place in dialogue with the rest of the community.

The member of the community, on the other hand, is also expected to know the spirit of the community and to interpret its laws in concrete situations. Moreover, this person is a focal point of the Holy Spirit, albeit within the ambit of the community's special charism as known in the founder and the community's constitutional expression, in seeking to know how to be responsive to the Spirit's urgings when making public decisions within the community. Eventually, the approval of the governor commanding or sending the person on a mission is needed. In the meantime, during the process of decision-making the person has recourse to the other members of the community, in particular the spiritual director.

Spiritual directors, therefore, do not make the decisions or send community members on missions. Their role is to be a source of light. They can help the person face disorders, enslaving attachments, and lack of freedom by recommending appropriate prayer exercises. These exercises may deal with personal sin or the desire to be with Jesus poor and humble. The spiritual director can also help to uncover evil tendencies operating under different guises. But in the decision-making process, the director will be of most aid in helping another person to judge the significance of consolations and desolations through the discernment of diverse interior movements. This assistance applies especially to the consolation resulting from the appropriating of the community's unique history in faith.

The spiritual director, if a member of the same community as the person being directed, has some advantage in the discerning process when decisions of an apostolic or lifestyle type are being made. The director is presumably a person who has appropriated the community's unique history, knows this kind of consolation and should then be able to recognize whether the direction of the inspirations is in keeping with the charism of the institute. The significance of the consolations and desolations are judged in terms of the experience of consolation that is given when the spiritual history of the founder and the order has been appropriated in faith. With a vocation decision, however, a member might find a freer spiritual director outside the order who can interpret the original vocation decision.

Generally, the positive signs of the Spirit's action will be those movements which strengthen the community, either by support or by challenge. The curve of the spirit described by Francois Charmot, S.J., is most helpful to a director in discerning the inspirations behind a person's decision making.

What are the stages in the evolution of states of soul that is guided by the good spirit, and what are those of an evolution led by the evil spirit?

The soul that is under the dominant influence of the Holy Spirit receives the first manifestation of this Spirit with "confusion"; then it feels itself to be "indifferent" that is to say, ready for anything that God may wish. It then experiences a profound peace, whatever happens. And, finally, it obeys with an unself-

ish heart, in spite of obstacles, a strong impulse to charity. This is always the action of the Holy Spirit on souls. It must be so if the director is finally to be persuaded that "the finger of God is here."

The procedure of the demon goes in the opposite direction. But before exposing it, we should further characterize the states of soul of which we have just spoken.

*Every inspiration and, all the more so, every vision or extraordinary voice, every project, every plan, every apostolic ambition which causes the idea to be born in the soul that it is preferred, chosen, elected by God for an exceptional virtue or for great work beyond the ordinary ought to be received by this soul with a deep feeling of confusion. This confusion should be sincere, spontaneous, and almost instinctive. (*Finding God in All Things, *translated by Young, William, S.J., Henry Regnery Co., Chicago, 1958, pg. 186)*

At times a spiritual director can support the member who is in the process of making representation to the spiritual governor on some issue. At other times the director will be a help for understanding the commands or mission of the spiritual governor.

As a member of a religious order I can come to conviction about a particular situation I am facing through the activity of weighing alternatives and prayerful discernment with the help of a spiritual director. Yet, I am to remain in a detached or free relationship to my conviction when I present my findings to the spiritual governor. This is an acknowledgment of the dimension that we have designated public or multilateral. The decision is still dependent on the action of the spiritual governor.

Now the role of the spiritual governor begins; the governor is in a position to decide and act upon the member's spiritual reflections and conviction or those of a group concerning the particular action.

Spiritual governors are not spiritual directors. They do not need to know in detail my prayer experience as my spiritual director does. They do not discern over my prayer experience. Yet, they should have some knowledge of my spiritual state when commanding me or when I am making an apostolic suggestion. Traditionally, this was the purpose of the "manifestation of conscience." In today's culture a sharing of my personal spiritual history, even if only in writing, can help my spiritual governor in discerning about me and my activity.

The spiritual governor employs the same process in making multilateral decisions as does the member of the community except that the field of consideration is different. The governor has to consider the ramifications of a decision with respect to the other members, weigh the alternatives, discern prayerfully, seek advice and spiritual counsel from others. With the spiritual governor the psychic and spiritual state of the member and of those a decision may affect is of high priority. The governor's own discernment will involve the consolation that comes when the request or command is in harmony with the consolation of the community's history. The validity of a request is thus recognized although implementation may have to be delayed because the rest of the community is not ready.

A difficult determination for spiritual governors is not only whether an insight or possible call to a member or local group is a good one but whether the member or local group will be able to carry it through. Here, I suggest, is where a knowledge of a member's or local group's spiritual history can be helpful to the spiritual governor as well as to the member or local group. What does this history say about the person's ability to carry through? What does it say about the Lord's way of using this person as an instrument for building his kingdom?

Of course, this same spiritual history can be an aid to spiritual governors seeking out the gifts in the community. This is an activity in accord with Paul's admonition:

There is a variety of gifts but always the same Spirit; there are all sorts of service to be done, but always to the same Lord; working in all sorts of different ways in different people, it is the same God who is working in all of them. The particular way in which the Spirit is given to each person is for a good purpose. One may have the gift of preaching with wisdom given him by the Spirit; another may have the gift of preaching instruction given him by the same Spirit; and another the gift of faith given by the same Spirit; another again the gift of healing through this one Spirit; one, the power of miracles; another, prophecy; another the gift of recognizing Spirits; another the gift of tongues and another the ability to interpret them. All these are the work of one and the same Spirit, who distributes different gifts to different people just as he chooses. (1 Co. 12:4-11)

In today's Church, spiritual governors will, no doubt, do much more dialogue than formerly with the person making a proposition. Still, they must make the final discernment over a decision and action. They are not the only discerners, but they are the final discerners. They give confirmation to an apostolic impulse by commanding or sending on mission.

The Necessity of Dialogue in Making Multilateral Decisions

Dialogue and representation in the making of multilateral decisions are of great importance for understanding the roles of obedience and mission in the challenge of today's world. They are also instrumental in attaining the consolation of history which in turn is so helpful in recognizing the correct decision and carrying it out.

This activity of dialogue and representation has a multifaceted apostolic significance: (1) it is important to the process for finding and carrying out an apostolic action; (2) it disposes the member to pass from the obedience of external observance only to willing obedience of the understanding, where one's mind and heart is in agreement with a decision because it is in harmony with the double appropriation in faith of one's own history and the history of the community (when the person can obey with such understanding this is indeed an experience of consolation); (3) dialogue and representation open the way for a fuller appropriation of the community's history; (4) this very communal approach is what the Church and the world needs today in the decision-making process.

As mentioned above, the present state of our culture is so complicated and changing that a member of a religious community is called upon more and more to make unusual decisions. The person's stance spiritually is quite different than it was 20 or 30 years ago. In the 1940's and 1950's a person's prayer might well be, "Lord, help me to do well what I know I am to do." Today, however, that person's prayer most probably is, "Lord, teach me to know what I am to do and give me the continuing freedom, insight, and strength to constantly adapt and meet the challenges of this changing world with authentic Christian decisions and actions."

I know myself as a member of a pilgrim people. If I am a member of a covenant community, my position is even more complicated because my personal decisions are multilateral in nature. True, I am not alone. I have support. I am able to communicate with my community in decision-making. The question before me is: "How am I to respond to the Spirit moving in me personally and still realize the multilateral aspect of my decision that my vow of obedience requires?" In certain cases this question becomes, "How can I experience the consolation of the community's history that carries me beyond obedience of execution and of the will to obedience of the understanding?"

This end is most often served by means of dialogue and consultation.

Traditionally, religious orders have allowed for discussion between a member and the spiritual governor through the practice of representation. In the past this was usually employed when someone objected to the command or initiative of the governor and generally had to do with a change of apostolate or place of residence. Basically, the person was expected to obey even though making representation. Representation was limited to a responsive role. It was seen as a help to fulfill an existing command more virtuously. It was meant to help the member move from an obedience of external execution to an obedience of the will in loving sacrifice of self, to an obedience of the understanding by which the whole person, mind and heart, could participate in the multilateral decision. In some instances representation gave the person the confidence needed to obey because manifestly "there was no sin in the command."

At times, even today, this responsive and somewhat passive attitude may be all that I can muster. It can help sustain me in patience until a more opportune time. But a spirituality in our times of social and cultural change requires more than this. Otherwise, frustration can build up and add to the already large residue of anger in people who have not been consulted for many years.

A more active role is expected of members of a religious order today. Initiative is a virtue. In some instances a spiritual governor may command a person outright. Then members can actually obey with alacrity or indicate by representation their objections to the command. But for the most part spiritual governors today tend to rule more tentatively; suggestions are made from both the members and the governor, and responses are elicited.

Within a covenant community, my own history and the existential situation may indicate a call both to me and to the spiritual governor. The call in turn moves me in the direction of action. This action is termed "mission." When the spiritual governor initiates a possible call there can arise within me as a result of prayerful reflection, an interior response to this initiative and possible mission. Then I am in a position to dialogue with the spiritual governor. My response to this initiative depends on whether my interior being is in harmony with the possible call and mission. The resultant dialogue takes place in a state of interior freedom on my part and on that of the governor, and future developments flow out of the dialogue.

A sense of call can also be initiated by the member of the community. The response comes in the experience of harmony or lack thereof in the governor's interior state as known through prior appropriation in faith of the different histories involved—that is, history of the Church, of the founder, of the whole order, of this province, of this community. The further step in the process—that is, commanding this activity or sending the person on this mission—is taken by the spiritual governor.

These kinds of dialogue are now considered important for proper decisions. This means that the member has an unavoidable responsibility to take a more active role in the community's decision-making. The governor should encourage this kind of initiative. Both are to be open to the lead of the Spirit as revealed by such dialogue. There is also a need that the community be indifferent or free in the process of making decisions. Yet, the position of authority remains so that after these kinds of dialogue, it is still the governor that sends the person on mission.

Both the governor and the member are to be responsive to the urgings of the Spirit, as discerned by the consolation in harmony with the sense of the community's history gained through faith-appropriation. Faith allows the member to be free, open, self-surrendering to the community's decision when the presence of its history is sensed. It allows the governor to respect the voice of the Spirit in the member living at the point of contact with the world when this voice agrees with this same consolation of the community's history. Both persons are trying to follow the lead of the same Spirit.

The appropriation of the community's history and its accompanying consolation makes for a more co-operative effort of seeking the will of God and responding to it. The member is no longer one against authority or something bigger than myself but a member of this covenant group. Together governor and member seek union of minds and hearts in struggling through dialogue and obedience to be one with the will of God in this enterprise of building his kingdom.

Simple and Sophisticated Methods

In all decisions in a covenanted group within the Church it seems there are three poles: the member or group of members, the governor or governing body, and the rest of the covenant group. Ideally, all three should be interacting but usually only two are—the governed and the governor. Still, the rest of the covenant group ought to be present affectively. Constitutions are updated to express the spirit of the founder for the present existential situation, in order to accomplish this purpose. But they do not always succeed.

There will be some decisions for individuals or for apostolic groups that can be made by a simple method and other decisions that require a more sophisticated method. The use of either method will be helped by the appropriation of the community's history in faith.

By "simple" method, I mean here that a member decides according to the customs and rules already in existence for coming to a decision, or the member asks and abides easily by the decision of a proper superior, who in turn applies the rules and customs with prudence. This simple method for coming to decisions within a community usually refers to the routine activity of living in a community or the running of an established apostolic work. The house customs, or common rules, or order of procedure already established are the norm. If the community and the members have truly appropriated the order's history in faith there will often be a simple, but important method of procedure for making this kind of decision. When the history and spirit of the order has not been appropriated in faith this simple method is often experienced as very abrasive.

In this simple method I readily consult persons in positions of authority and follow their decision easily and peacefully. I may find this use of authority quite helpful in certain decisions I am called to make. I and the one in authority have to decide if the simple method is sufficient for the decision at hand, or if a more sophisticated procedure is called for.

The more sophisticated procedure might follow a method similar to that given for unilateral decisions in Chapter 9. But now both my spiritual governor and I are called upon to weigh the alternatives and recognize the significance of interior spiritual movements. I may do this before or after making a request to the spiritual governor. Again, I must gain spiritual freedom in order to leave the governor free to make the final decision. As pointed out above, the appropriation of the community's history with its accompanying consolation will help me and the spiritual governor to recognize the urgings of the Holy Spirit.

This sophisticated method is important for decisions made by a group in a concerted setting. Such communal decisions involve a group of persons in dialogue with the spiritual governor. These may concern life-style and apostolates within the larger religious order or how decisions relate to the constitutions. Such communal decisions might use one or other of the methods of communal discernment now being practiced. Again, the final decision is given by the person with authority. It is good to remember that in the example of St. Ignatius and his first companions, the consensus to adopt obedience in a new religious order was dependent on a higher authority, that of the Church. In general chapters and other governing situations a group can determine the limitation of authority on decisions of lifestyle and apostolate made by individual persons, small groups, local communities and provinces.

The Consolation of a Community's History

In this sophisticated method the following procedure should aid the members and the spiritual governor in discerning true spiritual consolation. This is important since the moment for making authentic Christian decisions comes with true spiritual consolation. In each step the appropriation in faith of the community's history and spirit will be an aid.

An existential situation stemming from the needs, demands, or critique of the world's human community or from a local human community stirs up in a person or group of persons questions of decision and action. These questions are met by the message of sacred scripture, which reveals Jesus' value system, and by the spirit of a religious order as experienced in the founders and the order's reaction to historical situations. The affective experience of harmony in contemplating these three elements—existential situation, scriptural word and the community's historical spirit—constitutes both the procedure and the discerning sign of true spiritual consolation within a covenant community.

A community has the advantage of gifts and gifted people (*cf.* 1 Co. 12). If discernment for public decisions requires the harmonizing of experience, scripture and history, then the existential experience will come from those active in the apostolates. The return to scripture will benefit from the judgment of prayerful scholars who are steeped in the inspired word. The present and forward thrust of an order can use the prayerful reflection of canonists and historians.

Even in establishing the alternatives for making decisions, the appropriation of the community's history is important. What is the spirit of the founder, as found in writings and historical actions, on such an issue? How has the community responded in the past? Where has the community sinned or found grace in a similar situation in the past? How can one word the alternatives in keeping with the spirit of founder, constitutions and community history?

Now a faith-appropriation of the community's history can proceed. This will involve the activity of memory as I search for the pattern of God's relationship with the community, and take responsibility for the past (wholeness) while being open to the future. This activity will be of the same kind as described in Chapters 5-8. But the material will be the covenant group's unique history. Because it is an appropriation in faith, I will pray reflectively on the community's history and written documents hoping for an affective experience that is the consolation of my community's history. I will be aided by the community's historians. They are the ones who can explain the context of the beginnings and the development of the order.

The appropriation may proceed by means of comparison. When I have appropriated my own history in faith, I can compare it with the history of a local community and then with that of the total religious order. A small group can do the same. A further appropriation will take place as I compare my own unique history within the history of the religious order to that of the history of Christ and his Church (including the Old and New Testaments) and eventually the history of mankind. It must be remembered we are speaking of history here as understood in a faith context, that is, history as perceived in terms of sin-history and blest-history. Such use of the sophisticated method will lead to a position where I or a small group within the order, and the spiritual governor are in the affective state of heightened awareness for public decisions.

I will search for the pattern of life with God in these histories and its accompanying affective reaction. As I search, I am aware, for example, of the paschal mystery in Christ's life, that persecution brings vigor to the Church ("the blood of martyrs is the seed of Christians"), that the hardships of founders bring forth fruit. I compare these to my present life situation and to that of the group or order to which I belong.

In a sense of being whole I willingly accept the successes and failures, sins and good works of the past and respond to these with feelings of joy and sorrow. Jesus is my greatest boast, Avignon and Alexander VI my moments of embarrassment, apostolates to the poor, the sick, the uneducated or the outcasts, by my order, the past in which I rejoice. The sins of affluency, power, intellectual pride are the sources of sorrow. With John XXIII and various declarations of recent chapters, I can confess these sins to the world. In the glory of Christ and the founding saints I have hope for the future.

My openness to the forward direction of my life is now realistic but hopeful. It is seen in Jesus' resurrection after his death, in the history of the Church always moving forward from her sins, in the hope expressed by the founders' lives. Openness to the future will not allow us to return nostalgically to the state of the early Church with a kind of righteous fundamentalism. The challenge of Vatican II urges us to promote faith and justice among all peoples, to investigate the historical process, to use collegiality for making decisions.

The practice of appropriating the history of the order in faith fits with the fact that I discover myself to be in union with the human community and with this particular community. I discover that I grow into the future with this community. Appropriation of this history in faith helps me and the community in line with the forward direction of our history.

A Community Activity

The activity of appropriating a community's unique history for the sake of making correct decisions may be better done within a community experience. A family, a Christian Life Community or other apostolic group, a religious community of men or women may set up a series of prayerful exercises, reflections and sharing to bring about the appropriation of this community's history in faith in a more effective and affective way.

The following procedure might prove useful. Certain persons in the group are asked to investigate the spirit of the community as it has been known historically. These persons can then give an introductory presentation of different aspects of the community's history. After such a presentation by one or many persons, the participants consider prayerfully the significance of this history. This consideration can be made in conjunction with scripture that a director (facilitator) thinks is in keeping with the previous presentation. A suitable grace is sought from the Lord, for example, "I ask of the Lord for a deep-felt appreciation of how the history of the early founders was in keeping with the life of Christ and how this compares to my own life as a member of this community." Then after the reflective prayer—probably a mixture of consideration, reflection, *lectio divina*, meditation and even contemplation—the community comes together to share what they have found in prayer.

This kind of activity—presentation, personal prayer, sharing—can be done two or three times a day. That will depend on the amount of time the group can give to this appropriation, the length of the sessions and the physical and psychological state of the participants.

The topics of this kind of group exercise would be similar to those mentioned above, although the unfolding exercise will reveal other dimensions that enhance the experience and the appropriations. The communal presentation adds to topics such as these: the conversion experience of the founders, the early life style of the founders, the early apostolate of the founders, the writings and spirit of the founders, the history of the total community down the centuries, the history of this particular locality and this very group, the blest-history, the sin-history. A sense of fellowship is experienced when another person in the group presents the history and spirit of the community in a personal, affective way. Similarly, recalling the sinful as well as the blest history through the voice of another member of the community can give an appreciation that is not gained from reading.

The sharing of one's prayer over the history of the community fits with the dynamic of appropriation that is present in directed retreats. I am referring to the five elements in a directed prayer experience: (1) the matter of prayer; (2) the experience of prayer; (3) the reflection on this experience; (4) the articulation of this experience; and (5) the future prayer flowing from this experience. The matter for prayer has a living quality to it that is communal. The experience is personal prayer but in a communal setting. The reflection now includes the present setting of other members in the community praying over the same history. The sharing is an articulation in which the whole community is present. The prayer on implications for the future has a social component.

Such a methodology would probably be aided if a certain number of spiritual directors were present during this experience. If so, a much more effective comparison of one's unique history with that of the community's history can take place. This type of activity also makes possible some community expressions that the person alone cannot achieve. There can be a sharing of positive qualities that are found in the community at the present time in keeping with its history. A more affective entry into the sin-history of the community through specially designed penitential services is possible, and the Eucharist will highlight the place of Christ's paschal mystery in the history of the community.

THE ROLE OF THE SPIRITUAL DIRECTOR

The following comments are intended to help a director more fully develop principles in guiding others in the process of decision making that harmonizes with their own communal vocation. What has been written in previous chapters is presumed in these comments.

A. *The director's experience of appropriating the communal history*

When the one being directed is in the process of decision making which involves an apostolic action or a life-style change or any decision which has some connection with the community in which the person is living it is important that the decision be made within the context of the appropriation in faith of the communal history. Hence it will be helpful if the spiritual director shares the same communal history as the one being directed and has entered into the dynamic of appropriating this same communal history in faith.

B. Methods facilitating the appropriation in faith of one's communal history

A variety of methods can be used to help the one being directed compare his or her life history with the history of the particular congregation or community:

1. Various passages from the constitutions could be used as material for reflective prayer.
2. The prayer material might focus on one or other of the following:
   (a) general history of the congregation.
   (b) evident moments of the felt presence of God (blest history) in the congregation's history.
3. One might ask the person to pray reflectively over the present members of the congregation in order to appreciate their gifts and weaknesses and to appreciate one's own gifts and weaknesses in relationship to those of others.
4. The person might be asked to pray through the five points of the examen of consciousness on one's own personal experience of life in the congregation over, for example, the last two years.
5. The contemplation of specific events of the congregation's past much as one contemplates the events of Jesus' life; for example:
   (a) a Jesuit might be asked to contemplate the event of Francis Xavier being sent by Ignatius to India. The separation of Xavier from Ignatius did not destroy his union of mind and heart with Ignatius. Xavier would write to Ignatius with tears and on his knees.
   (b) a School Sister of Notre Dame might be asked to contemplate the event of the death of Mother Caroline in 1892. (An actual example of this type of

contemplation is given in Section E with permission of the writer.)

C. Encouraging the affective and contemplative element

As the one being directed begins to compare his life history with that of the congregation's history by remembering and searching meaningful events of the past, the director listens carefully to the affective nuances for the sake of encouraging the affective and contemplative elements of the prayer. If prayer is becoming too busy or too involved with problem solving, the director should encourage the person to be more relaxed and to allow the contemplative element to emerge. The director should encourage any type of prayer activity that is liable to aid the one being directed to be disposed for a kind of harmonizing consolation. For example if the event of the separation of Xavier from Ignatius seems to be the kind of event that would be meaningful to a Jesuit receiving direction, then the director would encourage repetitions of this same material in order that he be open for a kind of parallel consolation. When the one being directed is in that affective state of union of heart and mind that is paralleled in the Ignatius-Xavier event, then he is in the proper context for decision making.

D. Encouraging the method of contemplation

At times it is hoped that the person will be actually using the method of contemplation while praying over the communal history. To take the same example again, in praying over the historical event of Xavier being sent to India, the Jesuit in prayer may be brought into the presence of Xavier as he is writing a letter to Ignatius on his knees. When this sense of 'being there' occurs the director should help the one being directed notice it and encourage this approach in future prayer. In the Spiritual Exercises of St. Ignatius the method of contemplation is used as a tool for discernment. Here the method of contemplation can be used in the same manner:

1. A method in which interior spiritual movements become operative

2. A prayer disposing one for the experience of consolation which is the context for decision making in the Lord
3. A means of enabling one to reflect on oneself and compare one's own history with that of one's community history
4. Disposing one for the appropriation of one's history in faith
5. Disposing one for the experiences of openness and wholeness

E. Example

Appropriating my own history in light of our SSND history; occurred while praying on May 21 and May 22, 1977.

Prayed over "In fact God, who can read everyone's heart, showed his approval of them by giving the Holy Spirit to them just as he had to us" (Acts 15:8).

Found myself recalling my own history and sensing Jesus knowing me before I had come to the deeper consciousness of these days of workshop. This filled me with peace and a desire to rest in the Father's constant care for me.

But the Spirit moved me to recall a moment in our SSND history which has always been a painful memory for me. Our American foundress, Mother Caroline Freiss, was sent by her superior to Germany to ask for a mitigation of the Rule in 1850. She went without the proper letter of authorization from her superior. When she arrived at our Munich motherhouse, our Foundress, Mother Theresa Gerhardinger received her very cooly. She (Theresa) made Caroline live in the guest quarters of the motherhouse and would not allow her to have any visits with the motherhouse community. After a painful 6 weeks in this situation Theresa made Caroline superior of the American mission and sent her home with the hoped-for mitigation of the Rule. Much has been said in our history showing why Mother Theresa acted as she did, but basically I have had a feeling of hurt for Caroline over her treatment by Theresa. (and, it's part of the humor of God, that I have given talks explaining how Theresa was really protecting Caroline from a Canon Law at the time which stated that any missionary returning to her native land without proper authorization from her superior would be asked to leave the community. Isaac Hecker went through such dismissal from the Redemptorists. Needless to say, Theresa kept Caroline's visit a secret so that she would not have to dismiss her as well as follow through on her desire to make Caroline superior of the American mission.) However . . . as I moved into recalling this event, I found myself witnessing something of a reconciliation between Caroline and Theresa, a vague sense of forgiveness from Theresa to Caroline. But suddenly I was drawn into an overwhelming awareness that I, too, had been forgiven, not only by Mother Theresa, but by the entire community of SSND that I had been with during these past 7 years especially. In my naivete I had done many things that I felt Theresa would not have approved of. But when I saw her forgiving Caroline, I suddenly felt that she was forgiving me and in her forgiveness I felt the forgiveness of others living today whom I have hurt. I wept and will never forget the feelings of gratitude and awareness of the Father's CONSTANT care for me throughout my own history. It was also apparent to me that Mother Caroline was interceding before the Father for all of her American daughters whom she knew so well. I was aware that she understood us; our American desire for freedom and individualism and yet she understood because she has been misunderstood by Mother Theresa. Somehow Caroline became my mother in a whole new way. It seemed as if the plan of renewal in North America had been initiated by Mother Caroline, "who knew our hearts and gave us the same Spirit" that had animated her own life.

Basically the prayer ended with a deep sense of having been forgiven by our foundresses and by other living SSNDs.

EXERCISE

Recognizing the consolation of my community's history when I am making decisions

Introduction

Then some men came down from Judaea and taught the broth-

ers, "Unless you have yourselves circumcised in the tradition of Moses you cannot be saved." This led to disagreement, and after Paul and Barnabas had had a long argument with these men it was arranged that Paul and Barnabas and others of the Church should go up to Jerusalem and discuss the problem with the apostles and elders.

The apostles and elders met to look into the matter, and after the discussion had gone on a long time, Peter stood up and addressed them. "My brothers," he said, "you know perfectly well that in the early days God made his choice among you: the pagans were to learn the Good News from me and so become believers. In fact God, who can read everyone's heart, showed his approval of them by giving the Holy Spirit to them just as he had to us. God made no distinction between them and us, since he purified their hearts by faith. It would only provoke God's anger now, surely, if you imposed on the disciples the very burden that neither we nor our ancestors were strong enough to support? Remember, we believe that we are saved in the same way as they are: through the grace of the Lord Jesus."

This silenced the entire assembly, and they listened to Barnabas and Paul describing all the signs and wonders God had worked through them among the pagans.

Then the apostles and elders decided to choose delegates to send to Antioch with Paul and Barnabas; the whole church concurred with this. They chose Barsabbas and Silas, both leading men in the brotherhood, and gave them this letter to take with them:

"The apostles and elders, your brothers, send greetings to the brothers of pagan birth in Antioch, Syria and Cilicia. We hear that some of our members have disturbed you with their demands and have unsettled your minds. They acted without any authority from us, and so we have decided unanimously to elect delegates and to send them to you with Barnabas and Paul, men we highly respect who have dedicated their lives to the name of our Lord Jesus Christ. Accordingly we are sending you Judas and Silas, who will confirm by word of mouth what we have written in this letter. It has been decided by the Holy

Spirit and by ourselves not to saddle you with any burden beyond these essentials: you are to abstain from food sacrificed to idols, from blood, from the meat of strangled animals and from fornication. Avoid these, and you will do what is right. Farewell." (Acts 15:1, 2, 6-12, 22-29)

This is an example of decision-making in the early Church. It brings together an honest regard for the essentials of tradition and the remembrance of how the Lord has been working in the historical experience of this present community of faith. The community in Jerusalem was able to arrive at this difficult decision not only by seeking the Lord's light, but by recognizing the harmony of the decision with the consolation of its own unique history.

Suggested Approaches

I ask from the Lord the grace to know that I am part of my community's unique history and to experience the consolation of appropriating this history with my own. I seek this in order that I may be in conformity with this consolation when making decisions in and with my community.

I ask the Lord to help me remember, search, be whole to and open to my community's history.

I begin by recalling the founder's life (action and experience) and writings. Then I move to recall the history of the order, this province, this local community.

All the while or afterwards, I search in the Lord for the particular style of God's dealings with the founder and the order. I search through our sin history (scandals, lack of love and courage); through our blest history (apostolates, generosity, growth in the Lord). Do I see where exterior failure and suffering may have brought charity, conviction, apostolic success; or where exterior success and well-being brought disturbance and breakdown?

I pray to consider this history realistically so I will experience being whole in it. I seek to face and accept the human in it and be willing to suffer as this history unfolds.

As I seek openness, I compare my own unique history with that of the founder and that of the order, province, local community. I pray to be open to the direction I perceive in all these histories of which I am a part.

APPENDIX

This appendix is directed to those persons who are well acquainted with the *Spiritual Exercises of St. Ignatius Loyola* either as directors or exercitants. Its purpose is to show the significance of the activity of appropriating one's history in faith during the prolonged prayer experience of Christian decision-making that is the complete thirty-day Exercises. A knowledge of the previous chapters is presumed.

There have been many references to the *Spiritual Exercises of St.Ignatius Loyola* throughout this book. In this appendix I intend to indicate the connection of spiritual history to the Exercises in a more explicit manner.

The Historical in the Experience of the Exercises

There are many growth elements in the experience of the Exercises. There is a growth in the methods of prayer for the different states of the exercitant—consideration [23, 164-168], examination of the conscience [24-43], meditation [45-71, 136-157], contemplation [101-120, 158-161, 190-203, 218-225, 230-237], application of the senses [121-126, 227], choosing [169-189, 337-344], and three other methods [238-260]. There is the experience within each one hour prayer period—an act of offering, an act of reverence, recalling the history, placing oneself in the mystery, seeking a grace, using points, making colloquies. The instructions for contemplating the mystery of the Incarnation illustrate these various components of a single prayer period [101-109]. There is the movement from purgation to illumination to union in the four weeks as St. Ignatius suggests in his introductory notes [10]. This is a growth that is spread over a period of thirty days [4].

The historical is an important factor in the experience of the Exercises. This can be seen in the five daily prayer periods, in the daily examination of conscience, and in the interview with the director. In each of these what has happened over a period of time (a day, a week, thirty days) is considered important.

In the compass of a retreat day built around five periods of prayer the historical dynamic develops by means of Ignatius' review of prayer and by his technique of the repetition. The historical dynamic begins with an initial prayer experience which is then reviewed. On the basis of that review the retreatant returns to the original experience from a precisely focused point of view. This return to the experience is itself reviewed, and this review is again the basis for a more profoundly focused return. Each prayer period builds on the previous one as awareness is heightened and deepened. An historical development thus unfolds.

This development, as well as the practical concerns about recollection and generosity enters into the daily examination of conscience. Each day, through this fifteen minute exercise, the exercitant can gain a sense of historical development while he recalls the five prayer periods he has made.

In a more explicit way the historical is present in the interview with the director. In this time the exercitant articulates what happened in the prayer periods. Often this very articulation brings a heightened awareness of the historical to the exercitant. The director listens for many things in these accounts. What type of person is the exercitant? What is the effect of the past on the exercitant? What experience of consolation and desolation has the exercitant been experiencing? But, more specifically historical, what is the movement within a prayer period and from period to period and from day to day? From these the director discerns the movement of spirits and the exercitant's relationship with God at the time. A director may have this question in mind, "What is developing historically?" The director may then ask the exercitant to reflect on this movement and development as Ignatius suggests in his introductory notes [6,7].

In the important activity of the discernment of spirits the exercitant is advised to investigate the past to discover and offset the cause of desolation by "much examination of conscience" [319, *cf.* 321]. But the significance of the historical in the dynamic of discernment is more explicit in the Second Week. Ignatius instructs the exercitant to investigate the history of temptation to evil under the guise of good by carefully observing, "the whole course of our thoughts. If the beginning and middle and end of the course of thoughts are wholly good and directed to what is entirely right, it is a sign that they are from the good spirit. But the course of thoughts suggested to us may terminate in something evil, or distracting, or less good than the soul had formerly proposed to do" [333]. The exercitant is thus encouraged to take an historical attitude towards the movement of spirits being experienced. This practice of investigating the immediate historical pattern of thoughts that lead to something evil, distracting or less good, will often lead the person to a more detailed investigation of the history of temptation, sin and fruitless occupation. The purpose of this kind of historical investigation is "that once such an experience has been understood and carefully observed, we may guard ourselves for the future against the customary deceits of the enemy" [334].

This also applies to those self-authenticating spiritual consolations when one is not aware of the passage of time until after the experience. Ignatius refers to these experiences as "consolations without cause" [330]. While "there can be no deception" in such a consolation Ignatius insists that an investigation of the thought pattern after such an experience is necessary:

A spiritual person who has received such a consolation must consider it very attentively, and must cautiously distinguish the actual time of the consolation from the period which follows it. At such a time the soul is still fervent and favored with the grace and after effects of the consolation which has passed. In this second period the soul frequently forms various resolutions and plans which are not granted directly by God our Lord. They may come from our own reasoning on the relations of our concepts and on the consequences of our judgments, or they may come from the good or evil spirit.

Hence, they must be carefully examined before they are given full approval and put into execution [*336*].

In fact, one who makes a habit of examining and investigating the thought pattern flowing from desolation and consolation as experienced over a whole course of one's life attains a more sophisticated understanding of how one is tempted as well as how one is led by the good spirit.

The Historical in the Text of the Exercises

In the text of the Exercises St. Ignatius refers specifically to the historical when he speaks of using the memory to recall a mystery of Christ's life and the blessings of one's own life.

The memory is a vital tool in the Exercises. It is a help to me in getting in touch with the historical in the life of mankind, the life of Christ and my own life. In the Examination of Conscience, the First Exercise of the First Week, The Second Exercise of the First Week, the Review of Prayer, the Contemplations of the life of Christ and the First Point of the Contemplation to Attain the Love of God, the memory has an important and significant role.

There are two places in the Exercises where Ignatius specifically asks me to consider my personal history. These are in the exercises on personal sin and the Contemplation to Attain the Love of God: "I will call to mind all the sins of my life, reviewing year by year, and period by period" [56]; "to recall to mind the blessings of creation and redemption, and the special favours I have received" [234]. Thus my personal history is present at the beginning of the Exercises as I am put in touch with the saving power of Christ in all the details of my life. And recalling my personal history is to be the take-off point for appreciating and responding to the love of God for me. Remembering special events and persons in time is to be the method of being in touch with all my life.

In the First Week I am instructed to use my memory to recall the cosmic sin-history of mankind and its historical effects. There is also an historical dimension in the consideration of hell as Ignatius asks me to recall to memory those who were lost before the coming of Christ, during his lifetime and after his ascension [71]. In the Colloquy of the First Exercise (which dominates the First Week) I am to recall my history of love for Jesus as I imagine "Christ our Lord present before me upon the cross . . . I shall reflect upon myself and ask: 'What have I done for Christ?' 'What am I doing for Christ?' 'What ought I to do for Christ?' " [53].

In the contemplations of the Second, Third and Fourth Weeks, the First Prelude is to "consist in calling to mind the history of the subject I have to contemplate" [102]. This history is the scriptural account given in the gospels of the New Testament. Ignatius' understanding of a mystery in Christ's life is demonstrated in the Third Point of the Nativity: a mystery is not an isolated incident in Christ's life but is contemplated in terms of his whole life on earth. "This will be to see . . . that our Lord might be born in extreme poverty, and that after many labours, after hunger, thirst, heat, and cold, after insults and outrages, He might die on the cross, and all this for me" [116]. Moreover, I am to reflect on my own history as I contemplate Christ's history (*cf.* [114, 115, 194]).

The Exercises Gain a New Vitality

The four phases of remembering, searching, being whole and being open that go up to make the activity of appropriating my history in faith can give me a new appreciation of the Exercises. I will highlight where these four phases are most present in the Exercises and some of their significance. Lest there be some misunderstanding about the place of the four phases in the activity of appropriating and their significance in the Exercises this must be said: the Exercises of Ignatius are *spiritual* and hence totally dependent on grace, as are the four phases involved in appropriating one's personal history. The whole enterprise takes place in a grace-filled context of faith.

Remembering

The phase of remembering as understood in the appropriation of one's faith and as described in Chapter 5 affects the experience of the Exercises. This remembering arouses in the exercitant an attitude of hope so that the Exercises can proceed within a context of hope. The exercitant approaches the various exercises remembering the great deeds the Lord has done for mankind and "for me".

I think in particular of Jesus' death on the cross "for me" in the Colloquy of the First Exercise [53], and the activity of God to prevent all creation destroying me [60] while saving me from hell [71] as I remember my sin-history (both ancestral and personal) [56]. And I remember Jesus' life in the contemplations of the Second, Third and Fourth Weeks, as comprising the Trinity's great work of leading mankind to a higher form of life. The Exercises formulate that the intent of the Trinity thus: "Let us work the redemption of the human race" [107]; and I become as conscious that this cosmic love finds its focus in me. Thus, in the Nativity, I realize that all this is "for me" [116]. At the Last Supper I remember "that Christ suffers all this for my sins" [197]; throughout his passion I recall the "great affliction Christ endures for me" [203]. I am led to rejoice in Christ's resurrection and follow his example of consoler as I remember his triumph over sin and death and its significance for me [221, 224].

All this remembering is gathered together in the Contemplation to Attain the Love of God where I am called to share in the life of the Trinity [234]. Thus, "I will reflect upon myself" [234, 235, 236, 237] and my past and I offer my memory as I hope to re-experience my whole life with the Trinity whose love and grace are "sufficient for me" [234].

Searching

The activity of searching is clearly evidence throughout the Exercises. It is most evident in the Daily Examination of Conscience, the Review of Prayer, and the First Method of Prayer over the Ten Commandments and the Precepts of the Church. There is also a form of searching in the Colloquies of the Third Exercise of the First Week [63], in seeking the causes of desolation in the Rules of Discernment of the First Week [319], and in examining the movement to evil, temptation, distraction and desolation in the Second Week [333, 334]. I need to search in the Two Standards to recognize how the program of Satan and that of Christ are expressed in my own life [142, 146]. This also applies to the three descriptions of the devil given by Ignatius [325-27]. Searching is necessary to discover the riches to which I cling and from which I must be freed [157], as well as to express correctly the alternatives in the method of discovering and choosing what is more pleasing to the Lord [178-189].

When I am searching out the pattern of my experiences with God, I am enabled to achieve a further awareness. I search through areas of my life already explored, but from a new standpoint. I search through my sin-history for the expressions of God's merciful presence to me. I will search through my call-history for the gifts and talents and the ways God used me even through my faults and weaknesses. So I examine all my gifts, talents, virtues, sins, faults, weaknesses from the way in which God protects me, adjusts to me, and leads me, as I may discover from my history.

From the beginning I may wish to know God's pattern with me so that I can recognize its presence as I seek to make decisions in compliance with his urgings instead of "under the influence of any inordinate attachments" [21]. The First Week exercises introduce me to the pattern of God's forgiving and saving love for me personally. I may realize in the First Exercise that God has a special forgiving love for me as he did for David. But at what cost [53]! David's son died while he continued to live (2 S. 12:13-19). The Father's son, Jesus, died while I continue to live. Hopefully, I will live with a new sense of humility as David did. As I pray through the experience of my personal sin-history and grow in abhorrence for my sins, I see the pattern of those sins and my disordered tendencies in the eyes of God's protective and patient love. "I led them with reins of kindness, with leading strings of love." (Ho. 11:4).

With the Call of the King and the contemplations over the mysteries of Jesus' public life, a further element in the pattern of my life with God comes into view. I experience the persistent way in which he calls me forth to build the kingdom. Through my experiences in prayer—of consolation and desolation, of generosity and tepidity, of courage and fear, of humility and pride, of holding on to things and becoming free—I grow in knowledge of how the Trinity draws me forward. While I am being exercised to overcome enslaving attachments or general tendencies of my personality [157, 349, 350] I recognize other aspects in this free and continual relationship I have with the Trinity.

Contemplating the mysteries of Christ's passion, death and resurrection while remembering the offering of the Kingdom [98] and the Third Kind of Humility [167] I am led to recognize more acutely the unique way in which my life follows the paradigm of Jesus' life. I begin to see and accept the elements in my life that echo the insights of Paul: "About this thing, I have pleaded with the Lord three times for it to leave me, but he has said, "My grace is enough for you: my power is at its best in weakness" . . . that is why I am quite content with my weaknesses, and with insults, hardships, persecutions, and the agonies I go through for Christ's sake. For it is when I am weak that I am strong" (2 Co. 12:8-10). The elements in my life may not follow the physical sufferings of Jesus and Paul. Still, I may know rejection, failure and weakness before other human beings. Embarrassment and fear can be mine during the retreat itself, for example, when I am talking to my director or when I am celebrating the sacrament of reconciliation.

With the Contemplation to Attain the Love of God, I may discover the pattern of the Lord's unique way of giving himself to me as "I ponder with great affection . . . how much, as far as He can, the Lord desires to give Himself to me according to his divine decrees" [234]. I may enter into a further searching for the pattern of these decrees in my own life when I consider my history as an expression of the Trinity's presence in me [235], their labour for me [236], and their source of virtue in me [237]. So I will reflect upon my history that "I may in all things love and serve the Divine Majesty" [233].

Being Whole

As I search a sense of wholeness is experienced. "Search, and you will find" (Lk. 11:9). At first there is a wholeness that comes with gratitude as it is expressed in the colloquies of the

First Week when I appreciate the great compassion and kindness of God in his merciful forgiveness of me [61, 71]. Again, there is a wholeness that comes when I become aware that I am loved and accepted as I am for the Lord calls me to join him in the enterprise of building his kingdom.

Yet, the phase of being whole as I appropriate my history in faith is something more. I move from the dependence of a child who is always seeking the comfort of a father's arms to a mature dependence on the Lord calling me to take on adult responsibility. Such dependence means that I face realistically my limitations, sins and weaknesses and call upon the Lord for freedom, courage, light, strength and perseverance.

This latter sense of being whole influences my reaction to the questions of the Colloquy: "What have I done for Christ? What am I doing for Christ? What ought I do for Christ?" [53]. In that sense I may discover that my response is humble, mature, and hopeful. This is also true when I accept the call of Christ to me in all its rigor. I acknowledge the difficulty of the undertaking and offering suggested by Ignatius [95-98] at the same time that I realize this is the only realistic response. This feeling carries me into the contemplations of Christ's public life as I "ask for what I desire. Here it will be to ask for an intimate knowledge of our Lord, who has become man for me, that I may love Him more and follow Him more closely" [104]. The sense of being whole as it has come from appropriating my history in faith gives me a realistic awareness of sufferings and triumphs. This helps me to seek the grace of sorrow, anguish, tears and deep grief in the great afflictions of Christ [203] and "to be glad and rejoice intensely because of the great joy and the glory of Christ our Lord" [221]. As I pray to Attain the Love of God, my sense of wholeness will give me a new appreciation of God, the Lover, sharing with me, as I read that "the lover gives and shares with the beloved what he possesses, or something of that which he has or is able to give" [231]. With the awareness of being whole, "I will ponder with great affection how much God our Lord has done for me, and how much He has given me of what He possesses" [234]. I may realize that there is a whole history of God's bestowing his gifts on me as I consider how "God works and labours for me" [236].

Two remarks of Ignatius are important for this sense of wholeness. In the Introductory Observations the director is instructed to be brief in explaining the points of prayer. " For it is not much knowledge that fills and satisfies the soul but the intimate understanding and relish of the truth" [2]. In the Additional Directions the exercitant is encouraged to "remain quietly meditating upon the point in which I have found what I desire, without any eagerness to go on till I have been satisfied" [76]. Thus a director might discover that the sense of satisfaction or the lack thereof, stems from the retreatant's history and sense of wholeness as the prayer proceeds.

If I begin to get this sense of being whole, the acceptance of responsibility is accompanied by the experience of continuity. The sense of continuity is heightened in the First Week as I realize that I am still alive even though my sins should have destroyed me. In praying over the Call of Christ, this sense of continuity perdures as I recognize that Christ can do great things through me even though I experience inadequacy, fear and insecurity as I face the future. So, in the following of Christ I realize the humanity of Christ in a new way. His continual dependence on the Father for acceptance and love fills me with confidence that I may rejoice when experiencing his type of poverty, rejection and insults. This sense of continuity helps me to remain contemplating the passion and death of Jesus without anxiety or an undue haste to get to the contemplations on the resurrection. The four points of the Contemplation to Attain the Love of God only heighten this sense of continuity for I am encouraged to remember the continual blessing of my life experience, the presence of God living in me, the labors of God to sustain me and the continual activity of God working through me to build the kingdom of justice and love.

Being Open

Much of the prayer activity of the Exercises is intended to help me gain spiritual freedom so that I may be open to the call of Christ in the time of decision. This kind of openness is introduced in the First Principle and Foundation when I wish to become indifferent to all created things and "not prefer health to sickness, riches to poverty, honour to dishonour, a long life to a short life. The same holds for all other things" [23]. Openness is to be experienced when making a choice of a way of life: "Besides this, I must be indifferent, without any inordinate attachment . . . I should be like a balance at equilibrium, without leaning to either side, that I might be ready to follow whatever I perceive is more for the glory and praise of God" [179].

The personal presence of Christ leads me to further openness. St. Ignatius suggests it in the offering I make of myself at the close of the Kingdom exercise "to imitate Thee in bearing all wrongs and all abuse and all poverty, both actual and spiritual" [98]. Again in the Third Prelude of the Second Week contemplations he directs me to "ask for an intimate knowledge of our Lord that I may follow Him more closely" [104], indicating both the need of being open and the impossibility of being open apart from God's grace. Praying the Triple Colloquy of the Two Standards exercise also demands an openness as I ask to be placed under Christ's standard in the highest spiritual poverty and even actual poverty as well as "in bearing insults and wrongs, thereby to imitate Him better" [147]. If I pray for the attitude of the Third Kind of Humility I am seeking another kind of openness by choosing "poverty with Christ poor, rather than riches; insults with Christ loaded with them, rather than honours" [167]. And the offering in the Contemplation to Attain the Love of God is an expression of trust and openness to the Trinity's love for me [234].

The phase of being open to the forward direction which I perceive when appropriating my history in faith give a different nuance to freedom and openness, since the experiences of my own life are brought to bear on the matter being considered. I do not begin with a statement of perfect spiritual life (perfectionism) and then seek to live up to it. Rather, I bring my past experience to the material of prayer and understand my life anew. Thus, to some degree I have already experienced the opposites of the First Principle and Foundation: health-sickness, riches-poverty, long life-short life, honor-dishonor, in the appropriating of my history. This means that my openness and desire for more freedom and union with Christ begin with a realism that I didn't have before appropriating my history in faith and this openness can grow in realism during the Exercises. When I have done some appropriating in faith, there is an initial awareness of spiritual poverty, if not actual poverty, and some experience of insult and injury with Christ, perceived in my life. The offering of the Kingdom exercise, the Triple Colloquy of the Two Standards, the desire for the Third Kind of Humility, are now made in prayer with more conviction and sense of historical realism. Such offerings and desires are seen as a great grace even though they are mingled with fear and repugnance at the memory of former insults and injuries. The appropriation of my history in faith assures me that Christ will be present to me when my prayer is answered. He was there in the past, although it is only upon reflection that I realize his abiding presence. This new awareness that I have suffered with Christ in the past fills me with desire to experience suffering with him in the future. I can appreciate the experience of the apostles: "The Sanhedrin . . . had the apostles called in, gave orders for them to be flogged, warned them not to speak in the name of Jesus and released them. And so they left the presence of the Sanhedrin glad to have had the honour of suffering humiliation for the sake of the name. They preached every day both in the Temple and in private houses, and their proclamation of the Good News of Christ Jesus was never interrupted" (Ac. 5:40-42). This appropriation of my history, with its past physical and psychological sufferings, gives me a new openness to face the statement of the Third Week: "This is to consider that Christ suffers all this for my sins, and what I ought to do and suffer for Him" [197]. The experience of knowing that my life has been a sharing with God through the activity of appropriating it in faith makes the Take and Receive [234] at the end of the exercises a joyful expression of openness to the forward direction my life is taking.

The openness attained through the appropriating of my history in faith enlarges my perspective at the time of making a choice in the Lord [175-189]. My freedom does not open upon some imaginary future; it takes its rise in my past life, now appropriated and appreciated, and receives from it a direction into the future. As I weigh the alternatives which offer themselves to me, my choice is influenced by the pattern of my life projecting itself into my future. This pattern grows more luminous and complete, and the phase of being open to the forward direction of my life gained by appropriation of it, broadens the base for discernment. Moreover, my discernment gains in accuracy and assurance from my heightened awareness that my history is immersed in my relationship with God. Now I experience consolation arising out of the appropriation of my history, and it lends an openness and optimism to my search for what the Lord has in store for me.

The Significance of Appropriation for the Director

If, as a director, I am continually appropriating my own unique history in faith, then I will be more sensitive to this phenomenon in the exercitant; I will appreciate anew the Spiritual Exercises; and I will understand more deeply the instructions for the director which they contain. Having appropriated my history, my practice of direction will profit from a renewed study of the Introductory Notes, the Rules of Discernment of Spirits, Some Notes Concerning Scruples and the Rules for Thinking with the Church.

The director becomes doubly aware of the significance of the appropriation of one's life history. First, there are all the phases involved in appropriation: remembering, searching, being whole and being open. Second, in the appropriation or in its failure lies the experience of consolation or desolation with regard to the total life of the exercitant. As for the phases in the course of directing the Exercises I can discern whether the exercitant is engaged with those phases in the several exercises, day by day and week by week. Being sensitive to these phases in the exercitant, as well as the sensible presence or absence of God, I can observe the movements of consolation or desolation in function of the exercitant's perception of a total lifetime.

As director, I have to listen carefully that I may learn how the Lord has been dealing with the exercitant and may help to interpret his action. But I am also there as a source of encouragement and instruction in the art of remembering, searching, being whole, and being open.

Remembering

Does the exercitant actually endeavor to use the memory as a means of self-reflection or to avoid remembering? Is that reflection made in a spirit of hope, whether in the consequent experience there is shame and confusion, sorrow and tears, fear and repugnance, or love and gratitude, encouragement and joy? As director, I can encourage the person to remember sins, sufferings and fears, in the hopeful abiding love of God that has been experienced throughout life.

Searching

With what expectations does the exercitant begin the searching, to find hope and meaning or guilt and bondage? Does the searching become a self-centered exercise focused on a guilt complex or an unreal fantasy? Is the searching made real by a continuing reference to God's presence throughout the exercitant's life history? That realism is fostered when the object of search is the possession of a lax or scrupulous conscience [349-350]. The same effect is secured when the exercitant searches out the presence of consolation and desolation [319] or the enemy's tactics in tempting us at our weak point [327]. On a larger scale, it is valuable to seek out the most frequent manner and course of deception and temptation experienced over the years [333-334].

Being Whole

As director, I can recognize the phase of being whole as the exercitant in the First Week exercises and the Kingdom exercise faces the reality of sinfulness disorder, and limitation in the life of one called to serve with Christ. That reality also takes on a more accurate perspective in the light of the retreatant's historical experience of having been a source of grace for others. In explaining the causes of desolation and temptation

[7,8] I may have the exercitant consider when and where and how they happened. This consideration helps to distance oneself from the immediate experience and to grow in the sense of wholeness. How often reading the Rules for the Discernment of Spirits may also bring distance and peace! The exercitant realizes that this kind of experience has been around a long time before the exercitant's own history.

Explaining how to "act in a manner contrary to that of the enemy" [350] on the level of spiritual experiences also helps the person gain a sense of responsibility and continuity with one's history. I can advise a person whose search discovers a lax conscience to become more sensitive and one whose search finds a sensitive conscience to be more relaxed [349-350]. Similarly, for the person searching-out the reasons for desolation it is important that I encourage patience and the expectation of consolation. Conversely, I can urge the person in consolation to prepare for ensuing desolation. In the difficult exercises to attain freedom before decision-making, that is, the Two Standards, the Three Classes of Men and the Three Kinds of Humility, a consideration of how one has experienced poverty, insults and humiliation in one's past history is helpful. This applies also to the challenging commitment "to do and suffer" for Christ in the exercises over the passion. As a director, I am sensitive to the existence of this phase of being whole in the exercitant and can judge the consolations and desolations being experienced in the Exercises in a new way. Generally speaking, the harmony between a person's wholeness and unique history gives a surer norm for judging in decision-making.

Being Open

The places where I am more likely to notice the phase of openness coming from the appropriation of one's history in faith occur when the exercitant is praying over the Call of the King, The Triple Colloquy of the Two Standards, the Note of the Three Classes of Men [157], the Three Kinds of Humility and during the decision-making process given by Ignatius [175-189]. Ignatius expects openness to the call of Christ in the person making the exercises. He insists on the need for generosity [5], and allowing the creator to work immediately with the exercitant [2, 15, 16] so that a decision will be made without any inordinate attachment [21].

The phase of being open as a result of the appropriation of one's history in faith means the person has already had some previous experience of the results of this type of openness and is able to observe the forward direction in the pattern of life more quickly. Past experience with God forms the basis of trust and hope for the future. As director, I can clue-in on this past experience of the exercitant and be aware of its continuing direction during the different exercises that emphasize being open to the lead of the Spirit. In the decision-making process this openness to the direction discovered in the pattern of one's history is a positive sign of true consolation that I look for as the exercitant reveals the results of contemplation and prayerful decision-making to me.

Consolation and Desolation

Besides the existence of the four phases during the experience of the Exercises, there is the checking of consolations and desolations in the decision making process. This is basically a study of the movement of spirits as the exercitant goes through the different exercises from day to day and week to week. When an exercitant is engaged in the activity of appropriation true consolation follows. As director, I will continually encourage the exercitant to return to this consolation as a verification of a present desolation or consolation. (When the present experience harmonizes and is in continuity with the comprehensive consolation of one's history, it "may be compared to a drop of water penetrating a sponge" [335]. However, when the present experience does not harmonize and is not in continuity, it "may be compared to a drop of water falling upon a stone" [335].)

When the exercitant is not in the process of appropriation, I should be sensitive to a harmonizing of the person's historical experience gained through these days of retreat with the present consolations and desolations. Sometimes, as director, I will mention this directly and sometimes I will be quiet and wait.

Communal History

The Rules of Thinking with the Church are important for decisions during and after the Exercises. They express in Ignatius' words an affective love for the Mystical Body of Christ.

When a person is making a decision, I, as director, must keep this affective relationship with the historical Church before me as I listen to the prayer experiences of the person I am directing. Is the exercitant sensitive to historical continuity in the course of the prayer? Does the consolation being experienced agree with the general direction of the Church's life down the centuries? Is the person in touch with this part of our common history?

This historical connection with the Church and having her sentiments on issues—even though one may see oneself as part of the loyal opposition in terms of the governing body—is important in decisions within a covenant community approved by the Church. Such communities are approved by the larger faith community and dependent upon it. The connection is usually made and sustained through the vow of obedience. This in turn will take me, as director, to the written constitutions and history of the community of the person I am directing. The questions now in my mind will be of this nature. Does the person know and agree with the constitutions and spirit of the order? Does the person have an affective sense of the history of the founders? Does the person experience the sin history and blest history of the order down the years to the present decision making situation? Does this affective relationship extend to the Church and her history?

* * *

These points of relationship of the activity of appropriating one's history and the Exercises of St. Ignatius should help the exercitant and the director to be more in tune with the actions of the Spirit as the person is making decisions both within and beyond the Exercises. The Exercises are designed to assist the person to come into close union with the Trinity and in this state to make responsible decisions. The person brings to the moment of decision a total life history, including all the aspects of natural, psychological and spiritual ancestry. When this history is appropriated in faith, while making the Exercises, all these factors are brought to bear on the discernment to be made. Therefore, as director, I will find it helpful to be sensitive to the activity of appropriation that is taking place in the exercitant, especially as it assists me in judging the consolations and desolations that occur in the time of decision-making.